Panafrigen Press

Contents

To every child of African descent who ever felt invisible, this book is for you.

With all the love in the world,

I see you.

Black History didn't start with slavery.   It
started with Family. And goes back thousands of years.

Black History is Family History

Prologue

Why write a book specifically about genealogy for the young Black beginner?

To quote Dr. John Henrik Clarke (an eminent African American historian and a pioneer of Pan-African studies), "To control a people, you must first control what they think about themselves, and how they regard their history and culture. Once they've been made ashamed of themselves and culture, you no longer need chains to hold them."

For too many years, we have been told in any number of ways that we have no culture and even less history.

And that our lives as a people essentially began with slavery. None of that is even remotely true. As we continue to read and learn history for ourselves (not just taking the mainstream's word for it) we learn more every day about the rich legacy of our African forebears.

When it comes to genealogy, we heard the same story with a slightly different twist—that our genealogy starts with the end of slavery, and that there's no way we could ever go back any further than 1870. And well, most of us believed it because we didn't know any better.

Well, we're well into the 21st century, and now we do know better. But just like anything else, when it comes to researching Black genealogy, there's always a little bit more to the story.

Consider this: a poll from the Pew Research Center found that most Black adults in America are more likely than the general population to say that their racial background is fundamental to the way they think about and see themselves. Racial identity also affected a Black person's sense of connection with the Black community locally, in the US, and around the world. (You'll see a bit later why this is important).

Overall, 76% of Black adults said that being Black is extremely (54%) or very (22%) important to how they think about themselves. This was true even if the person identified as Hispanic or multiracial.

Additionally, 65% of the Black adults surveyed rated ancestry as also deeply important.

Black folks who hold their Blackness as fundamental to their identity were also more likely than other Black adults to see common ground with different subgroups (Caribbean, African, etc.) of the Black population. They also view what happens to any Black person anywhere in the world as something that affects them personally.

Another interesting element of this poll was that most Black adults had at some point had conversations with elder relatives about their family. Nearly 80% of Black Americans say they've spoken to relatives to learn about their family history—definitely more than the number who'd tried to learn via online research (34%), or by using a DNA kit (15%).

About half of the Black adults surveyed said they believed they were extremely or very informed about the history of Black people in the United States (51%), with another 37% saying they know a little something, and 11% saying they feel they don't know much at all. Those who feel at least a little bit informed are more likely to say they learned most of what they know from family and friends (43%) than from media (30%), the internet (27%), grade school (23%) or their college or university, if they attended one (24%).

These numbers tell us that African American history in general is primarily learned from family and friends. The internet and TV are a distant second with school bringing up the rear. This is sad, but not surprising. The good news is that this is absolutely in keeping with how our ancestors transmitted information via storytelling. So clearly, you are already part of a long tradition of learning from your family. Genealogy is just going to help you go a little further and create a system for how you collect and organize the information you have. And of course—tips to collect even more! Maybe you are thinking that this sounds nothing like the conversations your family has. That's okay. You can be the one to start talking about your family history.

This handbook does contain a fair amount of Pan-African and African cultural and social history. We included it for two reasons: 1) We recognize that Black history in most schools is often an afterthought at best, and nonexistent at worst and nowhere near comprehensive, and 2) Because of that, we believed it would be helpful to ground you (the new Black student genealogist) in a bit of our history as a foundational tool for furthering your interest in and research of, both Black history and your family history. Always remember that Black history didn't start with slavery. It started with family.

Genealogy is present in all you do—because it informs who you are. And when you learn the history of your family, you have the opportunity to live up to the expectations of your ancestors and choose to become the kind of person that future generations of your family are proud to look up to.

To paraphrase the words of Thea Bowman, a Black Roman Catholic nun, bring your whole self to this endeavor—all of who you are. Your history, your culture(s), traditions, your experiences. Embrace your identities. My guess is that as you go back and reclaim your ancestors, you'll discover one or a couple of them may have shared some of those very experiences and even identities.

Feel free to write in this book—on every page if you want. Highlight it. Use different colors. This book is from me to you. So anything that helps you read and remember is fine by me :)

Sr. Thea Bowman
(1937-1990)

Introduction

You may be wondering if that is an actual flag on the cover of this handbook. It is—it's the Pan-African flag (minus the kids of course). In the summer of 1920, two Black groups, the United Negro Improvement Association (UNIA) and the African Communities League (ACL) had a conference in New York and adopted the flag on August 13.[1]

The inspiration for the flag came from a 1900s so-called "coon song"[2] called "Every race has a flag but the coon". In a 1921 speech, (as printed in the weekly newspaper) Marcus Garvey was quoted as saying: "Show me the race or the nation without a flag, and I will show you a race of people without any pride...". Clearly, in his mind, what Black people needed was a flag.

The flag's colors carry a deep meaning as well. To paraphrase Garvey:

"Red is the color of the blood that people must shed for their redemption and liberty; black is the color of the noble and distinguished race to which we belong; green is the color of the luxuriant vegetation of our Motherland."[3]

Pan-Africanism[4] itself is an international movement that sees all people of African descent (indigenous and within the African diaspora of the Americas and Europe) as one people having a common origin, history, and culture (which the trans-Atlantic slave trade merely interrupted and divided). It aims to encourage and strengthen bonds of solidarity, and fight against colonialism, imperialism, neo-colonialism, and neo-imperialism in all its forms.

Lastly, Pan-Africanism focuses on the need for "collective self-reliance". That means that Black people should depend on themselves to take care of their needs. Well-known Pan-Africanists included Toussaint Louverture, Anna Julia Cooper, Fannie Barrier Williams, Ella D. Barrier, Haile Selassie, Kwame Nkrumah, Marcus Garvey, Amy Ashwood Garvey, Amy Jacques Garvey, Malcolm X, Claudia Jones, and W.E.B. DuBois. When you have some time, read up on these folks. They weren't perfect, but they believed in a cause or in an idea, and they fought for it. The seeds of the Pan-Africanism of the 1900s grew into the Black Nationalist and Black Power movements of the 1960s and 1970s.

So in genealogy, we used this flag to symbolize our connectedness as people of African descent. With each other here in the United States, but also in the Caribbean, in Central and South America, in Canada, and with Africa. We view our history—Afro/Black history—through a lens of empowerment, uplift, and joy. We can be proud because the strength of our ancestors ensured our existence.

If that's not resilience, what is?!

1. The flag was adopted as part of the Declaration of the Rights of the Negro Peoples of the World.
2. A type of song popular with white people in the late 19th and early 20th century that dehumanized African Americans.
3. According to the UNIA's Universal Negro Catechism.
4. As a philosophy, Pan-Africanism represents everything: the entire historical, cultural, spiritual, artistic, scientific, and philosophical legacies of Africans and African-descended people from the past to the present.

Chapter 1

Black Genealogical Beginnings

In 1976, a Coast Guard veteran-turned-author named Alex Haley published a

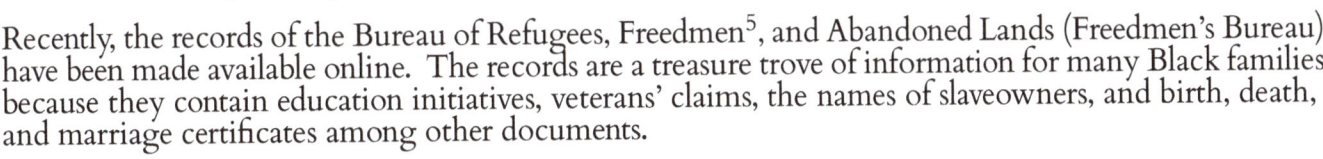

fictionalized account of one Black family in America from their beginning as kidnapped Africans in the 1800s through the Civil war to the 1970s. *Roots: The Saga of an American Family*, was later made into a television miniseries that ran on ABC in 1977. It was "must-see TV" at the time and opened America's eyes to a much more realistic view of the Black experience of slavery, the Civil War, Reconstruction, and the Civil Rights movement.[1]

It was this book, more than anything else, that really brought Black genealogy and family history[2] into the public eye. Black people all over the country began to trace their family history. Since *Roots*, several books about African American genealogy appeared, although not many of them were actually written by Black genealogists.[3] The problem though, was that trying to do Black genealogy was challenging at best and nearly impossible (if not actually impossible) at worst.

Alex Haley (1921-1992)

Traditional genealogical sources did not always lend themselves to the study of genealogy for Black families. For one thing, slaves were not legally considered actual people (remember that whole 3/5th's thing?[4]) So there are not many federal records of any kinds as they relate to Black people. Marriage between slaves was illegal, and those unions were rarely recorded before 1865. It was also illegal to teach slaves to read and write, so there are very few documents written by freed people in their own hand prior to the Civil War. Census records did not list slaves by name, if at all. Generally, they were denoted by their color (Black or mulatto) and age. Most slaves also did not have last names and so took the name of their most recent slaveowner. However, that may or may not have been the family that originally bought the slave.

Recently, the records of the Bureau of Refugees, Freedmen[5], and Abandoned Lands (Freedmen's Bureau) have been made available online. The records are a treasure trove of information for many Black families because they contain education initiatives, veterans' claims, the names of slaveowners, and birth, death, and marriage certificates among other documents.

It bears a mention that most records that will be of any use to the Black genealogist will be found in the local county courthouse of the county where your ancestors and relatives lived. Wills, probate records, land claims, bills of sale, etc., are found in the county or city courthouse. So as you get more serious about finding your lost ancestors, those records will be of particular interest to you.

So, given all that, why even bother trying to trace your family history?

Because it matters. It matters who you are and where you come from. Your identity is important, and the more you know about yourself and your family, the greater your sense of identity will be. We already know one thing about you: you're here. That means that you come from a family of survivors. And that is a great start.

You may ask: Well, what if my family is made up of people who didn't make good choices?

So what if it is? No one is perfect, and no one's family is made up completely of angels. Use whatever you learn to strengthen who you are. Look at the choices they made and ask yourself if those choices really work for who you want to become.

Maybe you can't be 100% proud of everyone in your family, and that's okay. But I bet there is at least one ancestor in your tree that you can look up to. Your mission: find that ancestor!

Only you can choose your future. Genealogy will help you understand your past so that you can make good choices in the present for a successful future.

You can do this!

And remember, it matters!

1. It is absolutely true that not every African brought to the Americas was a slave. If that is the case for your ancestors--then doing the research of your family history may be considerably easier--and that is awesome!
However, the vast majority were, so this book is written from the perspective of that reality.
2. Depending on where you stand, this may be a distinction without a difference, but technically, genealogy is the study and tracing of lines and descent. Family history is a record of relationships among family members that may include their medical histories.
You could say genealogy is the outline and family history is the essay.
3. Some of our Black genealogical forebears are: Charles Blockson, James Dent Walker, Delores Woodtor, Jean Sampson Scott, Frazine K. Taylor, Nova Law, Tony Burroughs, and Paul Crooks. There are also many African Americans who have written and published their family histories and created family history blogs.
4. In case you don't remember, the "Three-fifths Compromise" was an idea pitched at the 1787 Constitutional Convention in Philadelphia by a northerner, James Wilson, of Pennsylvania In an effort to get southern states to agree to a new government framework. The Revolutionary War had shown that the Articles of Confederation were lacking in many respects, as they didn't exactly create a union among the states. The agreement (Article 1, Section 2 of the Constitution) said that a slave would be counted as 3/5 of a free person to determine a state's total population. These numbers would then determine how many seats a state could have in the U.S. House of Representatives and also how much each state paid in taxes. The Constitution was ratified in 1788. Note: Slaves were not considered people, but were often referred to as chattel-as in chattel slavery. Chattel itself refers to movable goods property, not fixed like real estate.

5. Freedmen was a 19th century term to denote newly freed slaves--men, women, and children.
Note: We'll use this term with the understanding that it encompasses all genders and ages.

Chapter 2
Africa

There are 54 countries in Africa. It is important to recognize that each country is unique with its own culture, customs, languages, and traditions. Of course, there are some commonalities and similarities, but it is a holdover of colonialism to lump all African countries together as "Africa" with no understanding of the differences.

MAP OF **AFRICA**

It is also a mark of colonialism that most maps illustrate Africa as roughly the same size as South America, when it is actually about twice as large. The same way that everyone can list European countries is the same way that children of African descent should be able to rattle off at least ten African countries and know something about each of them. (Just sayin')

COUNTRIES OF AFRICA

Flag	Country	Capital	Languages
	Nigeria	Abuja	English Hausa Igbo Yoruba
	Ethiopia	Addis Ababa	Afar Amharic Oromo Somali Tigrinya
	Egypt	Cairo	Arabic
	Democratic Republic of Congo	Kinshasa	French Kikongo Lingala Swahili
	Tanzania	Dodoma	Swahili Arabic
	South Africa	Pretoria	English Zulu Swazi
	Kenya	Nairobi	English Swahili

Flag	Country	Capital	Languages
	Uganda	Kampala	English Swahili
	Algeria	Algiers	Arabic Berber
	Sudan	Khartoum	Arabic English
	Morocco	Rabat	Arabic Berber French
	Angola	Luanda	Portuguese Kikongo Kimbundu
	Mozambique	Maputo	Portuguese Swahili
	Ghana	Accra	English Dagaare Twi Ewe
	Madagascar	Antananarivo	Malagasy

Flag	Country	Capital	Languages
	Cameroon	Yaounde	French English Fula Ewondo Arabic Igbo
	Côte d'Ivoire	Yamoussoukro	French
	Niger	Niamey	French Arabic Buduma
	Burkina Faso	Ouagadougou	French
	Mali	Bamako	French Bambara
	Malawi	Lilongwe	English Chewa
	Zambia	Lusaka	English

Flag	Country	Capital	Languages
	Chad	N'Djamena	Arabic French
	Somalia	Mogadishu	Somali Arabic
	Zimbabwe	Harare	Chewa English Xhosa
	Guinea	Conakry	French
	Rwanda	Kigali	Kinyarwan French English Swahili
	Benin	Porto-Novo	French Fon Bariba Yoruba Dendi
	Burundi	Gitega	Kirundi French English
	Tunisia	Tunis	Arabic

Flag	Country	Capital	Languages
	South Sudan	Juba	English
	Togo	Lomé	French Ewe
	Sierra Leone	Freetown	English Krio
	Libya	Tripoli	Arabic Berber Tamasheq Teda
	Congo	Brazzaville	French Kituba Lingala
	Liberia	Monrovia	English
	Central African Republic	Bangui	French Sango
	Mauritania	Nouakchott	Arabic-Ber Pulaar Soninke Wolof

Flag	Country	Capital	Languages
	Namibia	Windhoek	English Afrikaans German Setswana RuKwanga
	Gambia	Banjul	English
	Botswana	Gaborone	Setwana English
	Gabon	Libreville	French
	Lesotho	Maseru	Sesotho English
	Guinea-Bissau	Bissau	Portuguese
	Equatorial Guinea	Malabo	Spanish French Portuguese
	Mauritius	Port Louis	English French

Flag	Country	Capital	Languages
	Eswatini	Mbabane	Swazi English
	Djibouti	Djibouti	French Arabic
	Comoros	Moroni	Comorian French Arabic
	Cabo Verde	Praia	Portuguese Cape Verdean Creole
	Sao Tome & Principe	São Tomé	Portuguese Forro Angolar Principense
	Seychelles	Victoria	English French Seychellois
	Somaliland	Hargeisa	Somali Arabic English
	Senegal	Dakar	French
	Eritrea	Asmara	Arabic English Tigrinya

Please don't fall into the Euro-centric trap of speaking disparagingly or negatively about Africa the continent, individual African countries, or African people. For far too long, many of us were only ever exposed to the negative aspects of Africa—corruption, disease, war, etc. While those things are real, it is also true that imperialists and colonizers had a vested interest in espousing the lie of African inferiority. By focusing only on the negative, we cheat ourselves of the opportunity of learning about the sheer beauty of the continent's individual and collective people, culture(s), and history(ies). This is our heritage, and we have every right to be proud of where many of our ancestors came from.

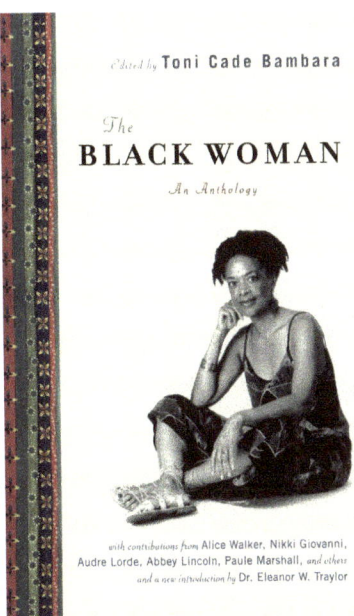

Edited by **Toni Cade Bambara**

The
BLACK WOMAN
An Anthology

with contributions from Alice Walker, Nikki Giovanni,
Audre Lorde, Abbey Lincoln, Paule Marshall, _and others_
and a new introduction by Dr. Eleanor W. Traylor

Author-activist Toni Cade Bambara attended the 1989 National Black Storytellers Conference at Medgar Evers College, Brooklyn, New York, where she proclaimed, "I know we must reclaim those bones in the Atlantic Ocean. Do you know there is not a plaque or memorial, a day, an hour that is erected in memory of those 100 million bodies in the bellows deep?"

Her words inspired the creation of the ceremonial remembrance now known as the Tribute to the Ancestors of the Middle Passage. While the first such official ceremony was held at Coney Island, New York City, in November 1989, these tributes have since spread all over the country, usually near a body of water. Generally, a libation[1] is poured first, then remarks are given by various community members, faith leaders, and politicians, then drumming and dancing. After that, the participants walk to the beach where they lay flowers at the surf's edge where many of our ancestors were lost (usually in) the Atlantic Ocean. These tributes serve to empower and uplift, because the participants recognize the sacrifices of the many people who came before.

---

1. A drink (water, juice, alcohol, etc.,) poured onto the ground or in a plant as an offering, tribute, or dedication. It is a way to remember and honor those who have passed away.

Chapter 3

Canada

Canada—the northernmost destination of the Underground Railroad. Just like the United States, our neighbors to the north have many people of African descent. Black history in Canada began with the arrival of Mathieu Da Costa[1], an Afro-Portuguese navigator and interpreter for Pierre Du Gua de Mons and Samuel de Champlain in the early 1600s. It's believed that many mixed-race African-Portuguese persons were part of the Atlantic Creole generation, often working as sailors or interpreters for European seafarers. In 2016, the Afro-Canadian population accounted for 3.6% of the total population. We are using the terms Black and Afro interchangeably to describe people of African descent in the Americas.

MAP OF CANADA

Africans arrived in colonial Canada as free people, indentured servants, and as slaves. British and French slaveowners began bringing African slaves to Canada in the 1500s. The buying, selling and enslavement of Black people was practiced by European traders and colonists in New France[2] in the early 1600s. There was a growing demand for enslaved Black people as a source of labor to avoid paying costly European workers. In 1689, King Louis XIV officially authorized the importation of enslaved Black people to New France. And by 1709, the French legalized the purchase and possession of slaves in New France and further solidified the institution of slavery.

NEW FRANCE

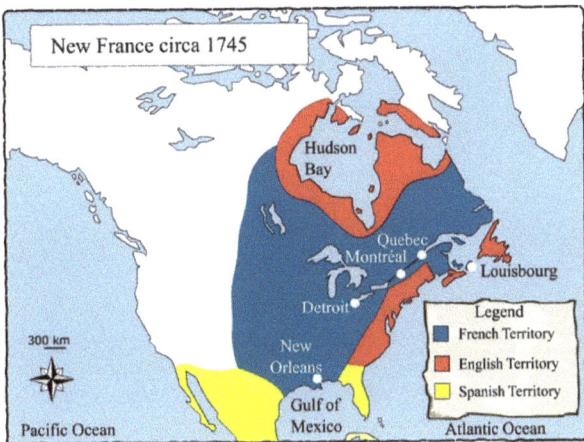

Free Black men and some former slaves in the thirteen American colonies (after fighting for the British) were resettled in Canada after the British lost the Revolutionary War. Enslavement expanded sharply in Ontario, Canada, following the American Revolution and was legally and socially accepted. In fact, Britain extended legal protection to slavery in British Canada to encourage settlement. The 47th Article of Capitulation of 1760 allowed French inhabitants to keep their slave property under British rule. The Imperial Act of 1790 encouraged settlers to bring the Black people they enslaved into the colony without having to pay taxes on them. Loyalists subsequently brought approximately 2,000 enslaved Blacks with them to Canada. Finally, many thousands of slaves escaped to freedom in Canada via the Underground railroad in the years leading up to the Civil War.

AFRO POPULATIONS OF CANADA

Provinces and Territories	Black Population (as of 2016)
Ontario	627,710 (4%)
Quebec	319,230 (3.2%)
Alberta	129,390 (1.4%)
British Columbia	43, 505 (1%)
Nova Scotia	21,910
Manitoba	30,340
Saskatchewan	14,925
New Brunswick	6,995
The Territories (Yukon, Northwest, and Nunavut)	1,350
Newfoundland and Labrador	905
Prince Edward Island	825

1. Da Costa was not the first person of African descent in Canada--he was just the first person whose history was recorded.
2. New France consisted of the colonies that covered a big chunk of North America, stretching from the Hudson Bay in the north to the Gulf of Mexico in the south.
3. These numbers are estimates, as many people classify themselves as mixed race.
Note: We are calling these African-descended populations "Afro" and not "Black" as Black is a term more closely associated with African-descended people of the United States.

Chapter 4
Central America

MAP OF CENTRAL AMERICA

It is interesting to note that in many "official" sources, some populations are classified as Creole[1] (may also be interchangeable with "mulatto") which is a term used to denote the descendants of slaveowners and enslaved Africans. If you didn't know that Creole meant Black, you would assume that some countries did not have any people of African heritage. To be fair though, the laws regarding intermarriage among the various ethnic groups was not quite as strict in Central and South America, so there are many communities where African culture is not really recognized as separate from the mainstream culture. Mexico is a good example of this. Additionally, Mestizo is a word commonly used to describe people of mixed European and indigenous (Native American) ancestry, but there can also be African heritage that is not recognized. Of note: Mexico did not recognize Afro-Mexicans as an ethnic minority until 2015.

AFRO POPULATIONS OF CENTRAL AMERICA

Flag	Country	Black Population	Languages
	Mexico	1.2% Black	Spanish
	El Salvador	0.1% Black 86.3% Mestizo	Spanish
	Honduras	2% Black 90% Mestizo	Spanish
	Costa Rica	83.6% Mestizo 6.7% Mulatto (can be another word for Creole)	Spanish Mekateliyu Bribri Patois
	Panama	9.2% Black 6.8% Mulatto 65% Mestizo	Spanish
	Guatemala	0.19% Black 56.01% Ladino/Mestizo	Spanish
	Belize	52.9% Mestizo 25.9% Creole	English Kriol Spanish

| | Nicaragua | 9% Black
69% Mestizo | Spanish
English
Miskito |

1. The word Creole is used interchangeably to describe both the people and their language. Creole languages include indigenous and African words, and has either English or a European language at its base. It is also called pidgin or patois.

Chapter 5
The Caribbean Islands

The Caribbean Islands were colonized by many European countries to include Britain, Spain, the Netherlands, and Portugal. However, not all of the islands had the right climate and soil for cash crops like sugar and coffee. On those islands, slavery still existed, but the slaves worked in other industries like mining, lumber, or shipbuilding.

MAP OF THE CARIBBEAN

Most slaves brought to the Americas were routed through the Caribbean first for something known as "seasoning". Seasoning referred to the process of Africans being forced to adjust or acclimate to their new status as a slave. If a slave didn't die after being introduced to the climate and the physical labor of slavery, they were considered seasoned, and were relocated to other colonies in the Caribbean, South America, and North America. In Brazil, a seasoned slave could sell for 15% more than one newly arrived from Africa.

AFRO POPULATIONS OF THE CARIBBEAN ISLANDS

Flag	Country	Black Population	Languages
	Haiti	95% Black	French Haitian Creole
	Anguilla (part of Great Britain)	85.3% Black	English
	Jamaica	92.1 Black	English Jamaican Patois
	British Virgin Islands	76.9% Black	English
	Turks and Caicos	88% Afro-Caribbean	English
	Aruba (part of the Netherlands)	75% Black (including mixed, mestizo, mulatto, multiracial) 10% Black and other ethnicities	Dutch Papiamento
	Bahamas	90.6% Black	English
	Curacao (part of the Netherlands)	70% Black (including mixed, mestizo, mulatto, multiracial)	Dutch Papiamentu English

	Barbados	91% Black	English Bajan Creole
	Dominica	86.6% Black	English Dominican Creole French
	Sint Maarten (part of the Netherlands)	Unknown	Dutch English Spanish
	U.S. Virgin Island	76% Black	English Virgin Island Creole
	Dominican Republic	15.8% Black 70.4% mixed	Spanish
	Martinique (part of France)	80% African	French Martinican Creole Antillean Creole
	Grenada	82.4% African 13.3% mixed	English Grenadian Creole
	St. Kitts & Nevis	92.5% African	English St. Kitts Creole
	St. Lucia	85.3% Black	English Saint Lucian Creole

	Puerto Rico	7% Black 49.8% mixed	Spanish English
	Antigua & Barbuda	91% Black	English Antiguan & Barbudan Creole
	Cayman Islands	24% Black 39% mixed	English Cayman Islands English
	Bonaire (part of the Netherlands)	85% Black	Dutch Papiamento
	Sint Eustatius (part of the Netherlands)	85% Black	Dutch English
	Saba (part of the Netherlands)	85% Black	Dutch English
	St. Barthelemy (St. Bart's)	Unknown	French English
	Trinidad & Tobago	36.3% African 24.4% mixed	English
	St. Vincent & the Grenadines	66% Black 19% mixed	English Vincentian Creole
	Montserrat (part of Great Britain)	88.4% African 3.7% Mixed	English
	Cuba	9.3% Black 26.6% mixed	Spanish Haitian Creole English

Expert Tip:

Geography is important—and not just for genealogy!

Chapter 6
South America

MAP OF SOUTH AMERICA

South America is much like Central America in the way that those of African descent are counted (or in some cases not counted). A few notes here: In Suriname, the word "Maroon" refers to the descendants of escaped slaves who intermarried with various other ethnicities. It is also interesting to note that Colombia has the second largest Afro population after Brazil. At one point Brazil had 134 (yes, you read that right) categories of race. Which is why it can be so difficult to actually count the population. Other official estimates put the mixed population at 43.13% and the Afro population at 7.61%. Chile's African-descended population was never officially recognized by the government. Finally, although the British explored the Falklands in 1690, and the French established a settlement in 1760 (that they eventually gave to Spain), no viable towns were built until the 1840s—after the islands were reclaimed by the British in 1833. By then, slavery had been abolished in all British-held territory.

AFRO POPULATIONS OF SOUTH AMERICA

Flag	Country	Black Population	Languages
	Guyana	29.3% African	English Guyanese Creole
	Suriname	21.7% Maroon-Bushinegue 15.7% Creole	Dutch Sranan Tongo
	Colombia	36-40%	Spanish English
	Venezuela	3.6% Black 51.6% Mestizo	Spanish English German
	French Guiana (part of France)	66% African	French French Guianese Creole
	Chile	4.7% African	Spanish
	Argentina	0.4-4.3% Black 83.6-96.6% Mestizo	Spanish Guarani Quechua

	Paraguay	65,000 Black 95% Mestizo	Spanish Guarani
	Uruguay	4.6-6% Black	Spanish Uruguayan Portuguese
	Brazil	49.6% Black	Portuguese
	Falkland Islands (part of Great Britain)	Unknown	English
	Bolivia	30,000 Black	Spanish Quechua Aymara Guarani
	Peru	5-10% Black 60% Mestizo	Spanish Quechua Aymara
	Ecuador	5-10% Black	Spanish Kichwa (Quechua)

PUEBLO TRIBAL AFRODESCENDIENTE CHILENO

LEY 21.151

In recent years, some Black and African-descended populations of the Caribbean and South America have begun to redefine what it means to be Black and to identify themselves as such in the movement towards greater visibility and inclusion. Discrimination based on skin color exists in most countries of the African Diaspora. Many groups fight for government recognition— because being seen is the first step towards equality. As we've noted, flags are symbols of unity, purpose, and vision.

Chapter 7

An American History Case Study - The Gullah Geechee

This is by no means a history book, but as we mentioned earlier, you have to be able to frame Black genealogy within the context of African and

European history. Every person of African descent—whether they arrived as slave, indentured servant, or free in the United States, the Caribbean, and Central and South America—originated from a specific country in Africa. And each of those countries had a rich history and culture.

As we noted earlier, most Africans who were brought to the United States were separated from their original group so that they would not have any ties to their homeland—either through language, religion, or culture.

However, in spite of that effort to erase African culture, there was one group that managed to maintain their cultural ties to the Motherland. And they remain the only known group of Black people in the United States to have formed their culture in relative isolation (from Europeans and white Americans) —a truly amazing feat.

Class is in session for five minutes— okay, maybe ten 😊

THE GULLAH GEECHEE

The present-day Gullah are descended from African captives who were brought to North America via the ports of Charleston or Savannah and lived in the coastal areas and sea islands of Georgia, Florida, South Carolina, and North Carolina. They developed a creole language called Gullah, and a culture with a pervasive African influence.

The Gullah people and their language are also called Geechee, which may be derived from the name of the Ogeechee River, near Savannah Georgia. Gullah is a term that was originally used to define the creole dialect of English spoken by Gullah and Geechee people. Over time, its speakers have used this term to formally refer to their creole language and distinctive ethnic identity as a people.

Queen Quet (Marquetta L Goodwine) Chieftess of the Gullah/Geechee Nation

According to Port of Charleston records, enslaved Africans shipped to the port came from the following areas: Angola (39%), Senegambia (20%), the Windward Coast (17%), the Gold Coast (13%), Siera Leone (6%), and Madagascar, Mozambique, and the Bights of Benin and Biafra combined at (5%). The term "Windward Coast" often referred to Sierra Leone, so the total figure of slaves from that region is higher than 6%.

Particularly along the western coast, the local peoples had cultivated African rice[1] for nearly 3,000 years. African rice is a lot like Asian rice, but there are differences. It was originally domesticated in the inland delta of the Upper Niger River. Once Carolinian and Georgian planters in the American South discovered that African rice would grow in that region, they often sought slaves from rice-growing regions because they had the skills and knowledge needed to develop and build irrigation systems, dams, and earthworks.

Two British trading companies based in England operated the slave castle at Bunce (Bance) Island located in the Sierra Leone River. Many of the slaves taken in West Africa were processed through Bunce Island. Slave traders sent many African captives to Charleston and Savannah during the mid- and late 18th century. Sierra Leone was at the heart of the traditional rice-growing region of West Africa where many of the Gullahs' ancestors originated.

It was a prime export site for slaves to South Carolina and Georgia. Slave castles in Ghana, by contrast, shipped many of the people they handled to ports and markets in the Caribbean islands for seasoning and re-export to other slave-holding areas.

Although the Africans were from different regions in Central and West Africa, they remained relatively isolated from whites while working on large Georgia and South Carolina plantations in rural areas. They were able to develop a creole culture that preserved much of their African linguistic and cultural heritage from various tribes; in addition, they absorbed new influences from the region.

The Gullah people speak an English-based creole language containing many African words. Gullah was also influenced by African language in terms of grammar and sentence structure. The Gullah language, sometimes called "Sea Island Creole" is similar to the Caribbean creole languages of the Bahamas, Guyana, Barbados, Belize, Jamaica (called patois), and the Krio language of West Africa. Additionally, Gullah crafts, farming and fishing traditions, folk beliefs, music, rice-based dishes, and story-telling traditions all exhibit strong influences from Central and West African cultures.

It's not clear where the word "Gullah" comes from. It's possible that it refers to Angola, where many of the Africans hailed from. They created a new culture synthesized from that of the various African peoples brought into Charleston and other ports. Some scholars have suggested that it may come from the name of the Gola, an ethnic group living in the border area between present-day Sierra Leone and Liberia in West Africa, another area of enslaved ancestors of the Gullah people.

MAP OF THE GULLAH GEECHEE HERITAGE CORRIDOR

FOODWAYS

The traditional Gullah Geechee diet consisted of locally available foods like vegetables, fruits, game, seafood, and livestock like goats, pigs, and cattle. Some products brought to the British American colonies from Africa during the slave trade included okra, rice, yams, peas, hot peppers, peanuts, sesame "benne" seeds, sorghum, and watermelon. Additionally, food introduced by Native Americans such as corn, squash, tomatoes, and berries made up the remainder of their diet. Rice became a staple crop for both Gullah Geechee people and whites in the southeastern coastal regions.

Making use of available foods, making a little go a long way, supplementing with wild game and fish, and using leftover parts that white people didn't eat (from butchered animals) were African cultural practices. African cooking methods and seasonings were applied not only in Gullah Geechee slave cabins, but also in plantation kitchens. Because plantation cooks were primarily enslaved women, much of the food today referred to as "Southern" comes from the creativity and labor of enslaved African cooks and their descendants.

Black food had historically been categorically panned by "foodies" because of its traditional reliance on unhealthy ingredients like lard (used because that was all the slaves were given to cook with). However, recently, it has begun to take its rightful place as elevated cuisine with thoughtful chefs who are staying true to the old recipes—but with healthy tweaks and substitutions here and there since hypertension, diabetes, and other food-related health issues do run in many Black families.

Chef Mashama Bailey practices what she calls "reclamation cuisine" which reconnects modern Southern cuisine with its African roots. Her skills have garnered attention: in 2019, Ms. Bailey won the James Beard Award for Best Chef: Southeast; the second consecutive Black woman to win the title. "Things changed [for my career] when I realized that my history mattered, my story mattered," Ms. Bailey noted.

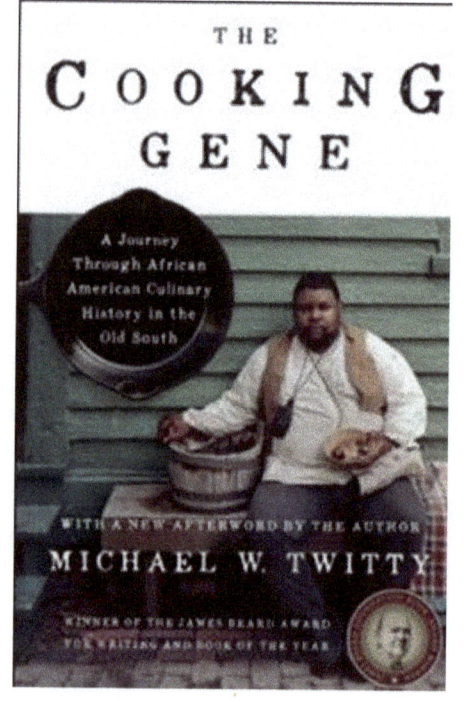

Chef and culinary historian Michael Twitty[2], author of *The Cooking Gene*, observed that, "There's this stereotype that black culture is a culture created on the fly, and that it's not rooted, and I think that's a very safe belief. That enables people who are outside of our world or community to be ignorant, because they don't have to learn the history, the tradition, the stories and folklore, or wrestle with the same emotional material that we do."

SPIRITUALITY

Religion and spiritual expression were fundamental in Gullah family and community life. Slaves were exposed to European Christian religious practices in a number of ways and incorporated elements that were meaningful to them into their African- based system of beliefs.

These values included a belief in God, community above individuality, respect for elders, kinship bonds and ancestors; respect for nature, and honoring the continuity of life and the afterlife. Lowcountry plantations frequently had a praise house or small structure where slaves could meet for religious services.

African culture also found its way into architectural designs in the Lowcountry[3]. Design magazines often attribute "haint blue" porch ceilings, doors, shutters, and houses to "coastal living." The truth is that the beautiful blue originated with Gullah Geechee people. The shade can vary from light blue to a deep rich blue, to resemble the sky or water (spirits have an aversion to water). The color is supposed to ward off evil spirits and keep them from entering a home.

When it came to attire, In the past, people often did not consider themselves fully dressed until they'd put on their amulet. It could be for good luck, to attract love, ward off evil, or reverse a hex. Amulets are herbs and/or roots sewn into garments, worn around the neck or wrist, or placed inside of shoes. Sometimes the secret mixture of herbs and roots is carried in a conjure bag or gris-gris. The bag is also referred to as a mojo, and the color of the bag symbolizes the desired outcome: green is for money, red is for love, and white is for a baby blessing.

talking to the dead

RELIGION, MUSIC, AND LIVED MEMORY
AMONG GULLAH/GEECHEE WOMEN

LeRhonda S. Manigault-Bryant

Some of the modern-day superstitions and rituals practiced in African American homes have their origins in Gullah-Geechee customs that are

sometimes rooted in the spiritual or religious traditions that enslaved Africans brought to the Americas. If you are like many of us, chances are you recall an elder mentioning some of the legends or sharing what was perceived to be a superstition. But more on African spirituality later. Incidentally, Daughters of the Dust, the 1991 movie by Julie Dash, is about Gullah culture. The movie is said to have been the inspiration for Beyonce's 2016 Lemonade video. Julie Dash was also the first Black woman to direct a feature film.

LANGUAGE

The Gullah people have several West African words in their language that survived despite over four hundred years of slavery when most other African Americans were forced to speak English. In the 1930s and 1940s, African American linguist Lorenzo Dow Turner did a ground-breaking study of the Gullah

language based on field research in rural communities in coastal South Carolina and Georgia. Turner, head of the English departments at both Howard University and later Fisk, identified over 300 loanwords from various African languages in Gullah and almost 4,000 African personal names used by Gullah people. He also found Gullahs living in remote sea-side settlements who could recite songs and story fragments and do simple counting in the Mende, and Fulani languages of West Africa.

For over 20 years, Turner made trips to the Gullah region as well as Sierra Leone in order to establish the link between languages there and the language spoken by the Gullah. In 1949, Turner published his findings in a book titled Africanisms in the Gullah Dialect that very quickly became the seminal work on the subject. Before Lorenzo Turner's work, White scholars viewed Gullah speech as substandard English, a hodgepodge of mispronounced words and corrupted grammar that uneducated black people developed in their efforts to copy the speech of their European slave owners. But Turner's study was so well researched and detailed in its evidence of African influences in Gullah that academics soon reversed course. It puts one in mind of the ebonics debate that raged in the 1990s. After Turner's book was published in 1949, scholars began coming to the Gullah region regularly to study African influences in Gullah language and culture.

Lorenzo Dow Turner
(1890-1972)

The Gullah phrase Kumbayah (come by here) became known throughout the United States and worldwide due to its inclusion in "Kumbayah", a song of the same name. The first known recording of the song was made in Darien, Ga., in 1926, and sung by a Gullah Geechee man named H. Wylie. The recording on wax cylinder was captured by Robert Winslow Gordon, the first head of the Archive of American Folk Song. The chorus was actually "Come By Here," which in the Gullah's Creole accent sounds like cum-by-yah. Over time, that pronunciation transformed into what we know today as kumbaya. The hymn was a call to God to come and help people as they faced oppression, danger, and violence.[4]

Expert Tip: This tip is not a knock on educators at all. Many are under various constraints with what they teach and how they teach it. Nevertheless, never assume that you are learning the true origins (or history) of anything—whether it's an invention, music, fashion, a dance, or a mathematical theory. It is always entirely possible (and often the case) that a Black man or woman (or other person of color) was the originator and that their idea or concept was appropriated and passed off as someone else's. As people of color, this is an unfortunate reality that we have to be aware of. This is why we have to do our own research. So that we know the real story.

1. The rice of Africa (Oryza glaberrima) has a long and noteworthy history. It was selected and established in West Africa centuries before any organized expeditions could have introduced its Asian cousin (Oryza sativa). It probably arose in the flood basin of the central Niger and prehistoric Africans carried it westward to Senegal, southward to the Guinea coast, and eastward as far as Lake Chad. Compared to its Asian cousin, African rice is better at tolerating fluctuating water depths, excessive iron, low levels of management, infertile soils, harsh climates, and late planting (a valued feature because in West Africa's erratic climate, the rains are often tardy).

2. Twitty's memoir offers a really thoughtful perspective on race and food culture. The book traces his ancestry--both Black and white--through food, from Africa to the American South.

3. The Lowcountry is a geographic and cultural region along South Carolina's coast, including the Sea Islands. The region includes significant salt marshes and other coastal waterways. Once known for its slave-based agricultural wealth in rice and indigo, crops that flourished in the hot subtropical climate, the Lowcountry today is known for its historic cities and communities, natural environment, cultural heritage, and tourism industry. The communities in low countries are still heavily dominated by African Americans communities, such as the Gullah/Geechee people.

4. For decades, the dominant narrative was that a white evangelist, the Rev. Martin V. Frey, had originally composed "Kumbaya." This story was spread in part by Mr. Frey himself, who got a copyright on the song in 1939, claiming to have written it in 1936 based on a prayer heard in Oregon.

Chapter 8

Umm…So Why Just Africans?

It is way beyond the scope of this handbook to try to get into the headspace of Renaissance, and later, so-called Enlightenment, Europeans as to why they not

only focused on Black slavery but also created an entire (and entirely false) narrative around Blackness. It wasn't like they'd never seen Black people before. Although, to be fair, most had not. But if you're interested, there are many excellent books on the subject of Africans living in Europe.[1] One of which is an excellent book, Black Africans in Renaissance Europe that discusses the experiences of Africans who lived in Europe during that time.

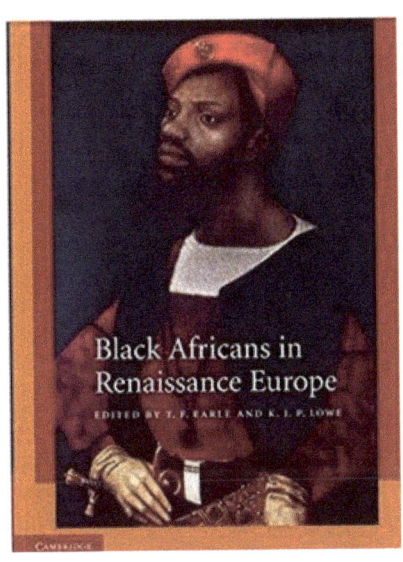

Kate Lowe, one of the editors, and author of one of the chapters, notes that the book explores how the main stereotypes concerning Black people established in this period. She provides several examples relating to the main set of prejudices, which were:

"…the African was generally identified as a naked person who would mutilate his/her face and body with scarification, piercings, and tattoos; he/she would be considered as carefree and characterized by immoderate laughter, unaware of his/her condition, lazy and sexually promiscuous, physically strong, a good musician or dancer."

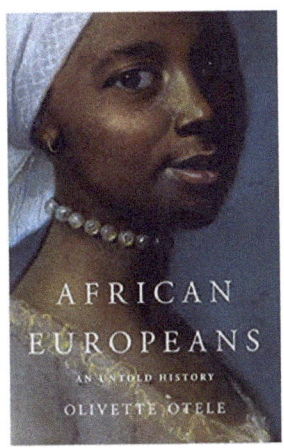

Lowe is basically saying that while there were noble and even knighted Africans in European courts, it suited the prevailing narrative (given the lucrative possibilities of slavery) to consistently describe Africans as "less than". That role was "necessary as a counter-image in the construction of European whiteness and 'civilization' (a notion coined in the eighteenth century)." The concept of "civilization" would go on to be one of the most misused and detrimental weapons in the European arsenal as it related to Africans.

Over time, words used to describe Africans were completely negative: barbaric, savage, uncivilized, godless, ignorant, heathen, animal…you name it.

Given that dynamic, it will probably come as no surprise that by the 17th century (1600s), it was easy for most Europeans and colonizers in the Americas to consider Africans as less than human; and pave the way for New World slavery to be defined solely by race. It may also have something to do with the fact that the New World (contrary to popular belief) was not completely colonized by law-abiding God-fearing citizens. In fact, for many years, European countries routinely sent the worst of their populations to the places like the United States. Criminals, debtors, outlaws, troublemakers, and heretics of all kinds often found their way to the U.S. Those people were already at the bottom of the social hierarchy, so having someone lower on the ladder than themselves allowed them to feel superior.

It is an unfortunate fact of human nature that most people like to feel like they are better than the next person in some way—whether it's money, looks, lineage, talent, etc. It provides a sense of security for insecure people. It is also a fact that the United States was a country that originated in violence. If you ever really study American history, you'll see just how violent it really is. From the very beginning, colonists were in conflict with each other, Native Americans, and the British. After the end of the American Revolution and the eventual genocide and/or removal of the Native Americans by the 1850s, they only had themselves and the Africans to contend with for the most part—at least in the homeland. But I digress. Fast forward to the present time, and you can see how 400 years of those kinds of words to describe Black people can become engrained not only in the people who use them but also the people who hear them. Recognizing and processing that generational trauma[2] on the collective Black psyche is necessary for healing. And genealogy can be a big part of that process of healing. But more on that later.

THE TRANS-ATLANTIC SLAVE TRADE

Europeans were familiar with Africa thanks to the African invasions of Spain and Portugal in 711 CE. The African general Hannibal's exploits against the Roman Empire were also widely known—at least in military circles. However, it wasn't until the 15th century that innovative sea-faring technology allowed Europeans to build ships that could handle the tidal currents of the oceans and allow for further voyages. Sub-Saharan African exploration soon followed beginning with the Portuguese, and it wasn't long before they were dealing in slaves. The first slave ship voyage to Brazil happened in 1526.

The biggest slave-trading European nations in order of volume[3] were Portugal, the United Kingdom, France, the Netherlands, Spain, and Denmark. It is interesting that three of the top six countries were the size of Connecticut. But what these countries lacked in size, they made up for with technological innovations in shipbuilding and navigation systems that allowed them to dominate the seas.

Slavery was an economic system. Many cash crops were extremely labor-intensive and required large numbers of people to work in very difficult climates. Slaveowners in the Americas grew crops like coffee, sugar cane, rice, indigo, cotton, and tobacco. Many slaves also worked in the precious metals, lumberyards, and salt mines of South America—and that was no picnic either.

It is important to note here that slavery, in one form or another, has existed since recorded history. Nearly every nation on the planet had engaged in a system of bondage, so it was not a new concept. Enslavement was also prevalent in Africa due to wars between neighboring African ethnic groups. However, Europeans did capitalize on, and in some instances, even instigate, those dynamics to foment wars between groups for the sole purpose of creating more slaves.

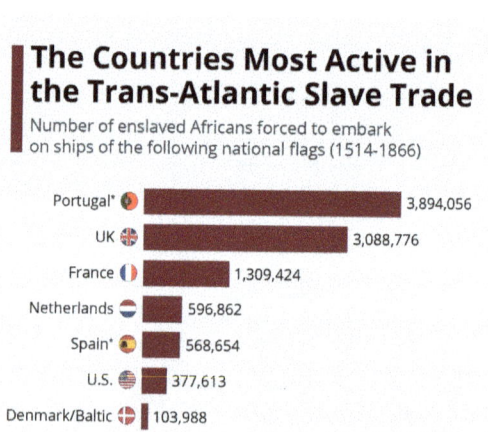

The Countries Most Active in the Trans-Atlantic Slave Trade

Number of enslaved Africans forced to embark on ships of the following national flags (1514-1866)

Portugal*	3,894,056
UK	3,088,776
France	1,309,424
Netherlands	596,862
Spain*	568,654
U.S.	377,613
Denmark/Baltic	103,988

FROM AFRICA TO THE AMERICAS

Remember too that kidnapping was not just conducted by the Europeans. While it is true that Europeans did kidnap Africans and crowd them aboard slave ships, it is also true that other African tribes went further inland and captured men, women, and children to sell them to the Europeans. There are very few innocent parties when it comes to the mechanics of the slave trade.

Africans were captured from various locations in Africa and brought to many areas in the United States, the Caribbean, and South America. The entire Trans-Atlantic slave trade[4] lasted from 1525-1866 and transported roughly12.5 million Africans. About 10.5 million Africans survived the Middle Passage.[5] And as you can see from the map, only a small fraction were enslaved in North America.

AFRICANS ENSLAVED BY REGION

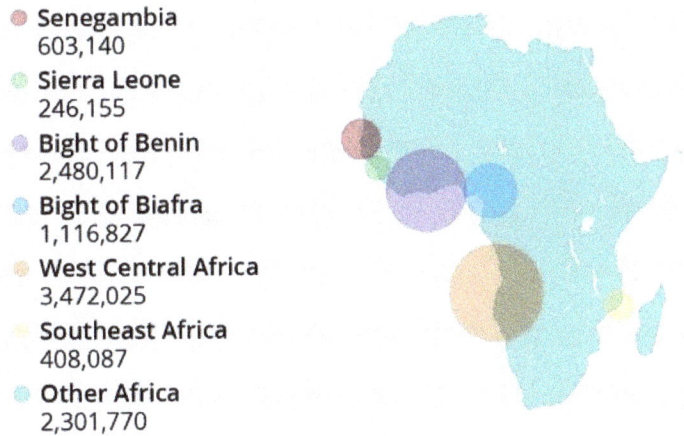

- Senegambia
  603,140
- Sierra Leone
  246,155
- Bight of Benin
  2,480,117
- Bight of Biafra
  1,116,827
- West Central Africa
  3,472,025
- Southeast Africa
  408,087
- Other Africa
  2,301,770

1. Other titles include Geraldine Heng, The Invention of Race in the European Middle Ages; Miranda Kaufman, Black Tudors: The Untold Story; Olivette Otele, African Europeans: An Untold Story; and David Northrup, Africa's Discovery of Europe.

2. Epigenetics (the study of how your behaviors and environment can cause changes that affect the way your genes work) has recently expanded to include the idea that trauma can leave a chemical mark on a person's genes, which is then passed down to future generations. See more in Chapter 16 on Reparative Genealogy.

3. Meaning the total number of slaves captured and shipped across the Atlantic Ocean.

4. These numbers are very rough estimates as there is no way to truly know how many people were forcibly brought to each location.

5. The "Middle Passage" refers to the trip across the Atlantic Ocean.

6. In geography, a "bight" refers to the curve of a coastline, bay, or other geographical feature-like a cliff.

Chapter 9
Slavery In the British Colonies

NEGROES
FOR SALE.

I will sell by Public Auction, on Tuesday of next Court, being the 29th of November, *Eight Valuable Family Servants*, consisting of one Negro Man, a first-rate field hand, one No. 1 Boy, 17 years o' age, a trusty house servant, one excellent Cook, one House-Maid, and one Seamstress. The balance are under 12 years of age. They are sold for no fault, but in consequence of my going to reside North. Also a quantity of Household and Kitchen Furniture, Stable Lot, &c. Terms accommodating, and made known on day of sale.

Jacob August.
P. J. TURNBULL, *Auctioneer.*

Warrenton, October 28, 1859.

Printed at the *News* office, Warrenton, North Carolina.

Slavery in the British-controlled colonies of North America and the Caribbean, and slavery in European-controlled countries of Central and South America evolved very differently. The decision in the 1772 case Somerset vs. Stewart, which had rendered enslavement illegal in England, did not apply to British colonies. In the British colonies, slaveowners made it a point to separate African people who were from the same tribes so that people could not communicate in their native tongue. Very often, families were sold and separated so that bonds wouldn't form. In fact, most Africans landed in the Caribbean first to undergo a period of "seasoning" which meant they were forced to accept slavery by a variety of violent and inhumane means.

As was previously explained, color quickly became the deciding factor in determining who was a slave and who wasn't. African slaves were not allowed to learn to read, practice their religion, travel without permission, etc. Soon, these customs became solidified into laws called Slave Codes. Given all the strictures mentioned, it is not surprising that within a few generations, many cultural aspects of the Africans' heritage like marriage, birth, coming-of-age ceremonies, etc., were lost.

In 1619, around 20 Africans landed in Port Comfort, Virginia. Kidnapped by the Portuguese from present-day Angola, they were traded to the British for food. Barely 20 years later, slavery in colonial American society became enmeshed with race and color. This was evident when in 1640, a Virginia court sentence handed down to John Punch stated that he was to "serve his said master or his assigns for the time of his natural Life." John Punch, along with two other servants, (one Dutch and the other Scottish) had attempted to escape from their employer and were caught. While each of the men received thirty lashes, the two white men were sentenced to serve out the remainder of their indenture, but Punch was given a life sentence.

A LITTLE MORE BACKGROUND ON SLAVE LAWS

None of the colonies' laws on slavery were drafted in a vacuum. In fact, there have been many academic articles published on the history of legal borrowing among the British colonies of Jamaica, South Carolina, Barbados, and others. Here is a quick rundown of some of the laws.

- 1639-40, Virginia: This statute created a legal distinction between white and black men.

- 1642-1643, Virginia: The fine print is that men of every color, and African women would be taxed; but not English women. The difference reflects that fact that Virginia's legislators believed that English and African women would play different roles in the colony.

- 1660, Virginia: This law, as it was written, indicated that some Africans and their descendants were not slaves.
  However, if a white indentured servant ran away with a black person who was considered a slave, the white servant had to serve additional time to compensate a master (or masters) for their absence and for the absence of the black individual.

- 1661-1662, Virginia: The fine print is that Indians and English indentured servants were to serve their masters the same length of time.

- 1661, Barbados: The Barbados House of Assembly passed two separate comprehensive labor codes aimed at better controlling their unruly labor force; one act governed "Christian Servants," (indentured servants), the other act governed "Negro" slaves. These acts codified racial distinction as a tool of mastery and served as a template for both Jamaican and South Carolina.

- 1662, Virginia: The fine print is that the child of an enslaved mother (and only African women were slaves) was also a slave for life.

- 1644, Jamaica: British colonists in Jamaica copy their slave code from Barbados.

- 1684, Jamaica: The Jamaica House of Assembly passed a new slave code with significant innovations.

- 1691, South Carolina: South Carolina adapted the Jamaican law.

The other British colonies took their cues from this early legislation and enacted similar laws in a relatively short amount of time. But don't think these kinds of laws occurred only in the southern states and the Caribbean:

- 1705: Massachusetts made marriage between blacks and whites illegal.

- 1706: New York declared Freedmen, Indians, and slaves who kill white people to be subject to the death penalty.

- 1706: Connecticut required that Indians, mulattos, and Black servants gain permission from their masters to engage in trade.

- 1708: Rhode Island required that slaves be accompanied by their masters when visiting the homes of free persons.

- 1710: New York forbade Freedmen, Indians, and mulattos to walk at night without lighted lanterns.

And those are just a few. It's also important to note that every British colony in the Americas benefitted from slavery. Even states with low or no

slaveholding populations profited from the labor of the enslaved. From sugar cane in Barbados to shipbuilding in Rhode Island, industries throughout all of the British colonies both supported either directly or indirectly, and were supported by, slavery.

California isn't a state that usually comes to mind when you talk about slavery. And yet, even though California entered the Union in 1850 as a free state (meaning the state legislature voted to make slavery unconstitutional), the reality is that as many as 1,500 slaves were transported to California between 1849 and 1861. Hundreds arrived before California became a state, but many others came after. The state was "free" only on paper—many of the people who settled the state (from the legislators on down) were from southern states and were determined to see the institution survive in their new home state. While slavery arrived in California the same time as the gold rush of the 1840s, but it stayed long after the rush was over. Through most of the 1850s, slaves could be found working in the gold fields and as house slaves in California. They often worked right alongside thousands of captive Native Americans.

THE

SLAVERY CODE

OF THE

DISTRICT OF COLUMBIA,

TOGETHER

WITH NOTES AND JUDICIAL DECISIONS EXPLANA-
TORY OF THE SAME.

Early white settlers in Oregon Country often held both anti-slavery and anti-black beliefs, and many came from states, such as Missouri, which had some version of exclusion laws. White settlers believed banning slavery would eliminate political controversy; but feared that settlements of freed slaves would compete for power with white people. One early migrant wrote that Oregon pioneers "hated slavery, but a much larger number of them hated free negroes worse even than slaves". He certainly was not the only one who felt that way. Even President Abraham Lincoln, as much as he disliked slavery, did not believe that Black people were equal in any way to white people, and wrote several times about how, if he could save the Union without ending slavery, he would do it.

In 1844, Oregon passed the first of three exclusion laws. It provided that a free black who refused to leave would be subject to not more than thirty-nine lashes. The law was promoted by Peter Hardeman Burnett, a Missouri settler who headed the provisional government's legislative council, and later became California's first governor.

The second law, enacted by the Territorial Legislature in 1849, was a flat prohibition against Black people coming to Oregon. At least one Black man, Jacob Vanderpool, was expelled in 1851. Three others were targeted, including Abner Francis, who wrote about Oregon's racial attitudes for abolitionist Frederick Douglass's newspaper. Francis and the others were allowed to stay, and the law was repealed in 1854.

The third law was written into Oregon's 1857 Constitution. It was approved overwhelmingly by Oregon voters —all white males — at an election in which the Constitution was also approved. Oregon thus became the only free state admitted into the union with an exclusion clause already in its Constitution.

George Washington (1817-1905)

The clause, which became Section 35 of Oregon's Bill of Rights, stated:

"No free negro or mulatto not residing in this state at the time of the adoption of this constitution, shall come, reside or be within this state or hold any real estate, or make any contracts, or maintain any suit therein; and the legislative assembly shall provide by penal laws for the removal by public officers of all such negroes and mulattoes, and for their effectual exclusion from the state, and for the punishment of persons who shall bring them into the state, or employ or harbor them."

Because of the law, George Washington, a Black man who'd been adopted by whites as a small child in Virginia, moved to Washington and founded a city he named Centralia. He is remembered as a leading Black pioneer of the American Northwest.

In 1852, Utah passed a slave code to protect the right of Mormons to hold Black people as property. New Mexico followed with its own slave code in 1859. Aspiring slave-holders in New Mexico could also enslave Native Americans, either by purchasing indigenous captives from slave traders or by trapping peasants in inescapable cycles of debt. The enslavement of native people in New Mexico was so deeply entrenched that it survived both the Civil War and the passage of the 13th amendment. Enslaved Native Americans could be found in New Mexican households late into the 19th century.[3]

---

1. You may see slave written euphemistically as "servant for life."
2. The statute was a total "about-face" from the previous seven or so centuries of English judicial law in which a child received their status from their father.
3. Holding people as property is also referred to as chattel slavery.

Chapter 10

Slavery in Central and South America (including the Caribbean)

In Central and South America, almost the reverse was true. While slavery was still horrific, people were allowed to remain in one place with their extended families. Cultural African traditions like religion, and even language in some places, remained strong and were passed down through generations. This is why, in places like Cuba and Brazil, there is such a very strong African influence (e.g., Yoruba) woven into the fabric of the culture of those countries.

The first documented Black person to arrive in the New World was an African from the Kingdom of Kongo.[1] Juan Garrido, who went to Portugal as a young man changed his original name to Juan,

and converted to Catholicism. It is unclear if he started out as a slave, a freedman, or a conquistador, but he arrived on the island of Hispaniola[2] in 1502. He later joined Ponce de Leon in 1508 on his voyage to Puerto Rico, and in 1513, he accompanied de León in his search for the Fountain of Youth and explored the area near St. Augustine, Florida. Six years later, he sailed with Hernán Cortés to Mexico where he fought the with the Spaniards against the Aztecs. By 1538, Garrido considered himself a conquistador (he also owned both African and Indian slaves), and wrote in his petition to receive money he believed was owed to him:

Juan Garrido (ca. 1480-1550)

"I, Juan Garrido, black in color, resident of this city [Mexico City], appear before Your Mercy and state that I am in need of providing evidence to the perpetuity of the king, a report on how I served Your Majesty in the conquest and pacification of this New Spain, from the time when the Marqués del Valle [Cortés] entered it; and in his company I was present at all the invasions and conquests and pacifications which were carried out, always with the said Marqués, all of which I did at my own expense without being given either salary or allotment of natives [repartimiento de indios] or anything else. As I am married and a resident of this city, where I have always lived; and also as I went with the Marqués del Valle to discover the islands which are in that part of the southern sea [the Pacific] where there was much hunger and privation; and also as I went to discover and pacify the islands of Juan de Buriquén de Puerto Rico; and also as I went on the pacification and conquest of the island of Cuba with the adelantado Diego Velásquez; in all these ways for thirty years have I served and continue to serve Your Majesty—for these reasons stated above do I petition Your Mercy."[3]

Garrido was certainly not the only one. During the 1500s, the Spanish and Portuguese routinely brought Africans aboard—as slaves, freedmen, servants, indentured servants, etc., to colonize the New World. In 1565, the Spanish brought slaves to St. Augustine, Fla., the first European settlement in what's now the continental U.S. In 1526, a Spanish expedition to present-day South Carolina was thwarted when the Africans on board staged a revolt.

---

1. The Kingdom of Kongo was an independent nation-state that existed from ca. 1390-1862. It was located in a region that encompassed portions of present-day Angola, Democratic Republic of the Congo, the Republic of Congo, and Gabon.

Note: Some historians list Esteban, or Estavanco (His real name was Mustafa Azemmouri) as the first African in the New World. Estaban was sold in 1522 by the Portuguese to a Spanish nobleman, Andres Dorantes de Carranza in the Portuguese-controlled Moroccan town of Azemmour. Mustafa was taken on the Narvaez expedition to colonize Florida for Spain in 1527. Of a crew initially containing about 600 men, only four survived to see the Mississippi River, the Gul of Mexico, and Texas. Mustafa was among the survivors.
2. Hispaniola is the proper name of the island that is comprised of the countries of Haiti and the Dominican Republic.
3. Juan was probably writing to the Viceroy of New Spain, Antonio de Mendoza y Pacheco, who held that position from 1535 to 1550. Note: Juan also claimed that he was the first to grow wheat in the New World.

Chapter 11

African History Keepers

We wanted to include a little bit about African culture—since it is the foundation for all cultures. The African oral tradition is well-known. Storytellers, known as griots, were some of the most important people in a family or village. Griots were the keepers of the family story and could recite the family group's history for many generations through stories, music, and song. Some griots were storytellers of the tribe and could tell and sing the stories of the tribe's entire historical record. The family stories including births, deaths, marriages, creation stories, wise sayings (proverbs), and myths. All this knowledge was passed down orally through each generation. It was an important way to stay connected to one's family and tribe. It also meant developing amazing powers of recall.

The African oral tradition is well-known. Storytellers, known as griots[1], were some of the most important people in a family or village. Griots were the keepers of the family story and could recite the family group's history for many generations through stories, music, and song. Some griots were storytellers of the tribe and could tell and sing the stories of the tribe's entire historical record. The family stories including births, deaths, marriages, creation stories, wise sayings (proverbs), and myths. All this knowledge was passed down orally through each generation. It was an important way to stay connected to one's family and tribe. It also meant developing amazing powers of recall.

The griot tradition began in the West African Mande empire of Mali in the 13th century. For centuries, designated griots told and retold the political, social, and cultural history of the empires, the tribes, and even the local village. If a person was a griot (and the position was hereditary), they would memorize the entire history of the village to include births, marriages, deaths. In this way, they also functioned as genealogists as well as historians.

It was their responsibility to pass on the stories so that the family stories are not lost or forgotten. Many griots play the kora, a long-necked harp lute combination with 21 strings. In addition to serving as the primary storytellers of their people, griots have also served as advisers and diplomats. Over the centuries their advisory and diplomatic roles have diminished somewhat, and they are now essentially seen as entertainers.

Chief Uwadiae Jacob Egharevba (1893-1980)

There were (and are) also African historians. One of the most important was Chief Uwadiae Jacob Egharevba (1893-1980). Descended from a high-ranking Benin official and a mother who was the granddaughter of a Yoruba chief from Ibadan, Nigeria, the young Uwadiae obtained his primary certificate and continued to educate himself as an adult with a fulltime job. He took a correspondence course through a London organization.

In 1914 he witnessed the coronation of Oba Eweka II in Benin City. The event inspired him to research and write a book that he hoped would "counter negative ideas about Benin and help recover memory of its 'power, greatness, civilization, and ancient culture'. His friendship with the new ruler (and his successor, Oba Akenzua II) allowed

him nearly free access to the royal court. He was able to interview priests of the royal ancestors who'd memorized generations of monarchs going back centuries, as well as other officials—both men and women. In addition to Edo oral histories and other sources, he compiled a history that was published in 1933 in the Edo language. It was translated and republished in 1934 as *A Short History of Benin* and became an instant classic. He later went to work as the curator of the Benin Museum, an institution founded by the British in Benin City.

By the time he died in 1980, he'd been blind for the last 30 years of his life but still managed to publish many books and pamphlets on Edo culture, history, literature, and art. Although he did work in a colonial organization, he managed to avoid the trap of dismissing African cultural practices and used Edo songs, biographies, fables, stories and proverbs as historical sources. He'd become a Christian many years earlier, but also engaged Edo divination practices.

1. The European equivalent would be a troubadour. The Japanese storyteller, the "hanashika", is somewhat different as they are more comedic and don't often directly reference historical figures or particular events. However, all ancient cultures have a storytelling tradition.

Chapter 12
African and Pan-African Spiritualism

Religion was fundamental to the traditional African way of life, although traditional African societies would have viewed their practices as less religious belief system and more as a cultural way of life. Broadly speaking, most tribes had a concept of a supreme God with a number of lesser deities that were more involved with human life. Many Africans also practiced ancestor veneration (worship) and animism.[1] Many believed that gods inhabited the natural world (trees, lakes, etc.) For many, praying to the ancestors was a logical course of action because it was the ancestors who could guide you and ensure you were on the right path. Additionally, many Africans practiced spiritism and divination.[2]

However, even before the slave trade, as noted in an earlier section, European travelers characterized Africans as godless and wicked. Given the propensity of most colonial white Europeans and Americans to view everything related to Africa through a lens of white supremacy, it is not surprising that African religions were also considered as less godly or spiritual than European Christianity.

That is even more surprising when one considers that Africa is mentioned early and often in the Bible. In the Old Testament, Moses was found by an Egyptian princess. In the first five books of the Bible, known as the Pentateuch, Africa is mentioned over 500 times. In the books of the major prophets, Africa or Africans are mentioned 180 times. Africa is spoken of by the prophet Jeremiah many dozens of times. In many contexts, Africa is portrayed as a refuge.[3]

Jesus and his parents fled to Egypt to escape King Herod. Egypt was actually the first African country to experience Christianity, as it arrived in the first century. It spread from there across northern Africa and by the fourth century, the ancient Aksumite empire in Ethiopia and Eritrea was one of the first nation-states in the world (if not the first) b to adopt Christianity as the official religion. That account is in the Bible in Acts Chapter 8. In that story, the Apostle Phillip meets an Ethiopian eunuch.

In the African tradition, he is named Qinaqis,[4] the treasurer for Queen Candace of the Ethiopians. Qinaqis had been in Jerusalem to worship (the implication

here is that he was an Ethiopian Jew) and was on his way back home. He was reading the Old Testament book of Isaiah when Phillip, who'd been told by an angel to take the road from Jerusalem to Gaza, happened by.

As the story goes, Philip meets Qinaqis and asks if he understands what he is reading. Qinaqis admits he doesn't, and Philip proceeds to tell him about Jesus. Qinaqis asks to be baptized, and then declares his belief that Jesus Christ is the son of God. Many of the early church fathers and mothers (many of whom were important theologians and philosophers) were African. Lastly, the Apostle Mark became the first African bishop in 43 CE (Bishop of Alexandria). Unfortunately, the history of African Christianity is not well known. By 1491, (whether for political or religious reasons or genuine conversion) the Kongo Kingdom in Central Africa had made Catholicism the state religion. The spread of Islam did reduce many of the Christian populations.

RELIGION IN THE NEW WORLD

With the onset of the trans-Atlantic African slave trade, concepts of European Christianity became more pervasive. Since most slaves were torn from their families, their cultural practices were forgotten within one generation. Either way, it is an established fact that spiritual practices, whether traditionally animistic or monotheistic, were extremely important to Africans. Slaves in the New World did everything they could to continue those traditions and practices—even if it meant hiding them under a veneer of European Christianity. We see this in practices in the Caribbean and South America with the proliferation of hybrid African/European religions. These include obeah in Jamaica and Santeria in Cuba, as well as those discussed in the next few pages.

VODOU

Probably one of the best known and yet most completely misunderstood religions is vodou (Voodoo in the US)[5]. Vodou originated in the ancient kingdom

of the Dahomey (present-day Benin, Togo, and Nigeria). The word derives from the Fon[6] word for "God" or "Spirit" and Is an organized, essentially monotheistic religion that incorporates both the energies of the natural world and supernatural forces. After the Haitian Revolution (1791-1804[7]), French planters brought their slaves with them to Louisiana, where the religion gained even more followers among the Africans and African Americans there and other areas of the American South.

Candomblé

Candomblé, meaning "dance in honor of the gods", is a religion that combines elements of ancient Yoruba, Bantu, and Fon religion with Catholicism and indigenous South American beliefs. Candomblé consists of one God, Oludumaré, and lesser but still powerful personal deities called "orixas" or "orishas" who control the physical world. One of Candomblé's teachings is that each individual is guided by an orixa who guides and protects them in their life. The religion is based on oral tradition and includes a wide range of rituals including ceremonies, dance, animal sacrifice,[8] and personal worship.

Rastafari

Rastafari[9] is a spiritual and socio-political movement that is a combination of Christianity, Pan-Africanism, and Ethiopianism, developed in Jamaica in the 1930s after Haile Selassie I was crowned King of Ethiopia. Rastafarians believe in one God, Jah, that lives in each person. Practitioners also believe King Selassie to be the second coming of Jesus and the reincarnation of God. The religion is decidedly Afrocentric and focused on the African diaspora. Some call for all Africans of the diaspora to return to Africa (also known as Zion or the Promised Land).

Rastafarian customs include following strict dietary rules, letting hair[10] grow naturally and practicing meditation. Rastafarianism drew world-wide attention during and after the life of famous Jamaican reggae artist Bob Marley.

Bob Marley (1945-1981)

Over the past ten years or so, the stigma against African-based religions is lessening. To summarize Stephanie Long from her 2021 article on the subject: Religion practiced by Black people throughout the diaspora is a combination—it draws on African worldviews about power, the spirit world, and the divine that is always in relationship with Christianity. For many, reclaiming ancestral practices is to assert Black agency[11]. It is a way of acknowledging our African heritage and culture, even if we didn't grow up with it (or previously viewed it through the dismissive lens of European Christianity). Black spirituality and Black culture continue to be the building blocks of personal identity.

In other words, Black spirituality affirms Black people, while discrediting and eclipsing aspects of Anglo American culture. As Ms. Long notes, "African American spirituality, by the way it shapes, informs, and strengthens Black life, creates a unique framework that accentuates the power, resiliency, and creativity of Black people. Spirituality, whether African Christian, African indigenous, or some mix, gave Black people the courage to create and construct a positive reality which has enabled Africans of the diaspora to develop resourcefulness and resiliency." Amen, sister.

Additionally, the scholarship on Black religion has expanded to include arguments for a uniquely African spiritual experience that includes both Christianity and elements of traditional African spirituality. Traditional Black spirituality. That's a mouthful. In the South, in the old days, it was called "Conjure". Many plantations had Conjure men and women who would make charms to protect slaves from punishment or help them escape—or both. Bottom line is—the two paths were not mutually exclusive, and many people today are going back to the old ways and forging a new spiritual identity that embraces both their African and American cultures…and their spirituality is the more meaningful for it.[12]

---

1. Animism is the belief that plants, inanimate objects (like rocks), and natural phenomena (like a lake or tree) have souls.

2. Divination is the practice of seeking knowledge about the future or the unknown by interpreting the layout of various small objects like leaves or bones in a standardized ritual.

3. The focus on Christianity, and not Islam, is because the United States, for all intents and purposes, was founded on tenets of Christianity (even if those tenets were so warped and distorted that no actual first-century Christian would recognize it as such...). Given how often the Bible was used to justify slavery, there should be no doubt about that.

4. In the European tradition, he is variously known as Simon Bachus or Simeon Bacchus.

5. For decades, Europeans and Americans have characterized this religion as evil. False narratives surrounding the religion include the primary purpose as being to cause harm to people with so-called voodoo dolls and hexes, and the creation of zombies.

6. The Fon are a tribe located in southern Benin,

7. Haiti, under the command of General Toussaint Louverture, was the first Black nation to overthrown colonialism in the Western hemisphere. And they have been paying for it ever since.

8. Similar to animal sacrifice in the Old Testament,

9. Also called Rastafarianism.

10. Hair in the Black community.

Books and movies (and terrible racist jokes perpetuated mainly by "us") have been written about the subject. Many of us were bullied as children because of the way our hair looked (or didn't look). Some of us were never told we had "good" hair. Because our families fell into the Anglo trap of equating "good" with "straight". And so we did our best to make our hair as straight and shiny as we could. Yeah, a great many of us have hair horror stories.

I'll just say here that basically, an Anglo marketing ploy convinced us that hair is supposed to be shiny and swingy and should take just five minutes to do. Why do we believe that? It's not even true for most white people. Our hair is so beautiful. And it deserves love and care and time and attention.

I have nothing against wearing pieces, fronts, wigs, etc. I want you to do you. My worry is just that many of us have internalized the view that our own hair is inherently ugly and shouldn't be seen. Even if we are wearing "natural" wigs with kinky hair.

If you've seen pictures from the 1970s and 1980s, a lot of white Americans--male and female permed their hair...to achieve that Afro look. Why? Because it is beautiful.

Its only recently that I have grown to truly see the beauty of my natural hair. I believe a lot of that comes from studying genealogy. When you spend enough time thinking about your ancestors, they become a lot more real. And somehow, they help ground you into your heritage and culture and identity. And that is empowerment at its best.

When I look at my hair now, I see the women who came before me. Women who may or may not have been allowed to tend to their hair in the ways they'd done in the Motherland. Women who were forced to figure out new ways and means of keeping their hair healthy. Because healthy hair is good hair.

I went natural about seven years ago and last year, I put my hair in braids. But in that year, I realized two things. One was that the only reason I turned to braids was because of some idea buried deep in my subconscious that my natural hair just "out" was not beautiful. That I needed the structure of braids for my hair to be considered acceptable in its natural state.

The second was that my hair, on its own, is actually gorgeous. That those tight little curls are truly things of beauty. That I don't have to struggle with it, or straighten it, or believe the lie that natural hair is so hard to manage.

Recently, I wore my hair in a "fro-hawk". My hair is about shoulder length, so it took some maneuvering and a few hair pins to keep it in place. And yeah...I got some looks as I rode my bike to run a few errands. But the affirmation I received was just...humbling. One Black man I passed actually said, "God bless you," in the most reverent tone anyone has ever spoken with to me.

So please don't buy into the nonsense that hair doesn't take time to style. It's okay to take time with your hair and learn what it likes and what works for it. But no matter how you wear it, just know that your hair is beautiful. When you look in the mirror, I hope you can see the beauty of your ancestors in your hair: the love, the strength, the joy in the texture, the color, the curl pattern, all of it. A big part of loving yourself is learning to love your own hair. Do not ever be ashamed of it. And promise me that you will always believe that any hair you have on your head that is healthy is "good" hair.

11. Agency here is defined as the ability to take action; to make one's own free choice.
12. See Yvonne P. Chireau, Black Magic: Religion and the African Conjuring Tradition.

Chapter 13

Adinkra

We wanted to include a section on Adinkra[1] symbols because they speak to the way in which values, moral codes, principles, and standards were communicated in the tribal cultures of Ghana. Adinkra symbols are decorative—people incorporate them into designs on clothes, pottery, and jewelry—but they also convey traditional wisdom and beliefs. There are over 50 symbols of the Adinkra; not all are listed here. We just wanted you to be able to recognize these sacred symbols when you see them.

SOME ADINKRA SYMBOLS

Symbol	Akan	Translation	Meaning
	Gye Nyame	Except God/ Only God	Symbol expressing the deep faith the Akans have in the Supreme Being
	Nyame Biribi Wo Soro	God is in the heavens	Hope and reminder that God's dwelling place is in the heavens
	Adwo	Calmness	Peace, calmness, and ppiritual tranquility
	Dwennimmen	Ram's horns	Humility and strength together—emphasizing that even the strong need to be humble
	Ananse Ntontan	Spider's web	Wisdom Creativity The complexities of life
	Nkyinkkyim	Twisting	Depicts the twists and turns of life and the need to be versatile and resilient to survive

Symbol	Akan	Translation	Meaning
	Denkyem	Crocodile	Adaptability Cleverness
	Adinkrahene	King of the Adinkra symbols	Represents charisma and leadership
	Asase Ye Duru	The earth has weight	Symbol of providence and the divinity of Mother Earth
	Menso Wo Kenten	I am not carrying your basket	Represents self-reliance and economic self-determination
	Sankofa	Go back and get it	Expressed as a mythic bird that flies forward while looking backward with an egg (symbolizing the future) in its mouth
	Kuronti ne Akwamu	Two councils of state	Represents democracy, sharing ideas and taking counsel.
	Mmere Dane	Times change	No condition is permanent whether it be good or bad. So the fortunate should not boast and the less fortunate should not give up

1. In Akan (Twi), the term adinkra refers to a particular type of cloth historically worn by royalty and spiritual leaders for important ceremonies.

Chapter 14
The Rise of Black Studies

While the Civil Rights movement was fundamental to Black Americans gaining their political rights, it had an added consequence of making many who'd never previously believed that Black people had a history worth mentioning—let alone studying—come to the realization that they'd been shortchanged educationally. Even after Reconstruction, when schools were set up for the newly freed slaves, the prevailing notion was that Blacks had no history and that nothing (good) had ever happened in Africa. However, new voices were rising up, and a new Black consciousness was developing. Social justice activism, the powerful voices of Martin Luther King Jr. and Malcolm X, the beginnings of the Black Power Movement, and the anti-war protests for the Vietnam War, all these things coalesced to ignite young people of color. When Muhammad Ali,[1] who had been drafted to fight in the war declared,

Martin Luther King Jr. (1929-1968) and

Malcolm X (1925-1965)

Muhammad Ali (1942-2016)

"My conscience won't let me go shoot my brother, or some darker people, or some poor hungry people in the mud for big powerful America. And shoot them for what? They never called me [the n word], they never lynched me, they didn't put no dogs on me, they didn't rob me of my nationality, rape and kill my mother and father. … Shoot them for what? How can I shoot them poor people? Just take me to jail."

Ali was arrested and stripped of his heavyweight title and banned from boxing for three years. New York suspended his boxing license and issued a $10,000 fine. He was convicted at trial in 1967 and found guilty of refusing to be drafted—which was a felony charge. But he remained free as his case would through the court system. Eventually, the Supreme Court overturned the conviction in the 1971 decision Clay v. United States.

As Al Sharpton later noted:

"For the heavyweight champion of the world, who had achieved the highest level of athletic celebrity, to put all of that on the line—the money, the ability to get endorsements—to sacrifice all of that for a cause, gave a whole sense of legitimacy to the movement and the causes with young people that nothing else could have done. Even those who were assassinated, certainly lost their lives, but they didn't voluntarily do that. He knew he was going to jail and did it anyway. That's another level of leadership and sacrifice."

Colin Kaepernick (1987 -)

Almost 50 years later, another professional athlete made national news by taking a stand—first sitting, and later kneeling, during the National Anthem to protest racial inequality, social injustice, and police brutality in America. He didn't have to go to court over it, but as of yet, he has never played for another professional team. His peaceful act of resistance was met by the mainstream media as an act of defiance against a country that "gave him everything". Even now, we shouldn't be surprised that the act is still mischaracterized as some sort of disrespect against the flag, the armed forces, and even America itself. But we have to understand that people will always have their own agenda when it comes to how we are viewed. Often times, "these are the breaks."[2]

By the late 1960s, in response to the growing demand of Black students to learn their history, many of the large colleges and universities created Black Studies departments. In fact, the very first Black Studies program was the result of a longstanding student strike at San Francisco State College (now San Francisco State University), led by the Black Student Union and the Third World Liberation Front.[3] The students demanded an Ethnic Studies program as well as an end to the Vietnam War. It was a major news event for weeks in the aftermath of Martin Luther King Jr.'s assassination. The strike ended in March 1969 with an agreement to create the school (now College) of Ethnic Studies, in which the Black Studies department was located.

More than 500 programs existed across the United States by 1971. In those environments, Blacks were able to learn more of their history, and develop a better understanding of the African past. Unfortunately. much of that history still isn't taught at the grade school level in quite the same way as White American history, so most students must do a lot more outside reading to get a clearer picture of the Black (or any ethnic) contribution to American history.

---

1. Muhammad Ali's was born In Louisville, Kentucky and given the name Cassius Clay by his parents. He changed it after his conversion to Islam and never answered to Cassius Clay again.
Note: Ali once said, "I should be a postage stamp. That's the only way I'll ever get licked." Interestingly, while other countries have honored him in this way, he does not have a stamp in the U.S.
2. "The Breaks" was a 1980 single by rapper Kurtis Blow. It was the first certified gold rap song.
3. In 1968, in response to growing demands for reform, a coalition comprised of the Black Students Union, the Latin American Students Organization, the Filipino American Collegiate Endeavor (PACE) the Filipino-American Students Organization, the Asian American Political Alliance, and El Renacimiento, a Mexican American student organization, formed at San Francisco State University (SFSU) and called themselves the Third World Liberation Front.

Chapter 15

Reparative Genealogy, Restorative Justice, and Resilience

Some define reparative genealogy as the "act of researching our heritage, acknowledging our connection to slavery, and "daylighitng" the history of those our ancestors enslaved. They note that while we cannot change the past, what we can do as genealogists (of any ethnicity), is take it upon ourselves to not only find slave-era family records, but to make those records available online to other researchers. As they note, "engaging in this form of repair connects the present to the past."[1] In this way, families researching their ancestors can be made more whole because they now have access to information that tells a bit more about their family history. So even if you are a Black researcher, if you find that your Black ancestors owned slaves (and there are many documented instances where this happened), make that information available so that others can complete their own story. You can't change what your ancestors did—and you'll be lucky to even find out why they did it, but you can make the effort to publish those records so that other families can begin to heal as they do their own research and come across your records collection. If we are truly serious about dismantling white supremacy in every way possible, doing honest and truthful genealogy is an excellent way to begin. That is reparative genealogy.

Cynthia Erivo (1987 -)

As we said earlier, for too many years, Black people (and other people of color) were stereotyped in extremely negative ways. And it can be difficult not to internalize those kinds of stereotypes when they are constantly in front of you. Even when it's not real, it can be disturbing.

Award-winning actress and singer Cynthia Erivo noted how when she played the character Celie in the Broadway revival of "The Color Purple", that being told "You're ugly" during each performance—at two performances a day and five days a week for months, took a toll. And she is gorgeous and amazingly talented as a singer and an actor!

But when you hear something often enough, it's really hard not to internalize it and start believing that maybe it's true—even when it's only part of your job for awhile. So we can understand how those of us who hear (or have heard) that, or worse, from people we don't know, or people we do know, may have had a seed planted in us that we somehow aren't good enough. Or smart enough, or pretty enough. But it's up to us to reframe that picture and see ourselves for the beautiful, brilliant, innovative, and wise (people with a past and a future!) humans that we truly are. Many aspects of our past were stolen from us, but we don't have to allow our present and future to be robbed too.

We also previously talked a little bit about epigenetics. The idea is not new. As early as 1912, Sigmund Freud (1856-1939) contended that the "archaic heritage of human beings" contains "memory traces of the experience of earlier generations." His theory focused on phylogenetic[2] endowment and the idea that we inherit our ancestors' experiences, and that those experiences form part of our subconscious. In his later works, he was writing about Jewish collective memory as it related to the Holocaust, the calculated genocide of at least six million Jews under the Nazi regime.

Carl Jung (1875-1961) took the idea a step further with his concept of the collective unconscious:

"…a form of the unconscious (that part of the mind containing memories and impulses of which the individual is not aware) common to mankind as a whole and originating in the inherited structure of the brain. It is distinct from the personal unconscious, which arises from the experience of the individual."

So as you can see, this idea of how the past can inform the present is valid and deserves a lot more study. Maybe you'll be the one to take it on…

You can't measure pain, in the sense of whose is worse. Pain is pain and trauma is trauma. Whether that brutality occurred repeatedly for 400 years before suddenly ending in 1865 (even though it really didn't), or a one-time multi-year horrific act of state-sponsored slaughter of an entire ethnic group (the Holocaust), the systematic removal and genocide of Native Americans, or the forced internment of Japanese in American labor camps during World War II. You also can't tell someone to "get over it". People are individuals and experience emotions differently.

Neither Freud nor Jung expanded their theories to really include the Black Diaspora, as both saw African-descended people as "less than." While earlier studies focused on evolutionary psychology and cognitive neuroscience, epigenetics has also shown that environment can influence emotional wellness. Without getting too scientific, the upshot is that while collective memory can't actually change your DNA, it can change the way your DNA reacts to certain things. However, all of this study is still very controversial and not exactly proven fact—by scientists anyway.

So take your time with this handbook. Think about what you read, and make notes of things you want to learn more about, either from your family members, or your own research.

And remember, it's okay if you have to be your own superhero.

You should know going in that not everything you discover will be great. It may not even be something you ever want to share with anyone else. And that's okay. Everyone has hard things in their lives. Maybe it's violent, or tragic, or traumatic, or all three. But whatever has happened in your family, even if no one talks about it, still impacts who you are—even if you don't know it or realize it.

So don't be afraid to ask questions. But do always be respectful even if family members don't open up right away, or ever. People cope in different ways, and sometimes resilience is a hard-won battle. And victory may be fragile.

Both good and bad experiences can shape who we are. But sometimes, when the experiences aren't great, it can be tough to move past them. And believe it or not, even though we are several generations removed from slavery, the trauma of it can be inherited, just like your eye color, or preference for almonds over pecans. Unlike those other two though, trauma goes deeper and can be much more difficult to recognize. According to Nia West-Bey:

"Historical trauma refers to a complex and collective trauma experienced over time and across generations by a group of people who share an identity, affiliation, or circumstance.

Cultural trauma is a related concept and occurs when members of a group feel they have been subjected to a horrendous event that leaves indelible marks on their group consciousness, forever marking their memories and changing their future identity in fundamental and irrevocable ways. Both historical and cultural trauma are lasting legacies of oppression identified by young adults in underserved communities as substantial threats to their mental health." [3]

Take time to process everything you learn—the good and the bad. If you can talk to older relatives, or a trusted adult, and explore some of the things that you know have happened in your own family. Sometimes just talking about things helps you see that they aren't the end of the world. And that while they may not be fixable, at least they are manageable. You can recognize that while your family history is a part of you, it doesn't have to define you if you don't want it to. Remember, you always have a choice. As you study African American history and your family history, you'll get a much more complete picture of not only our struggles, but our moments of joy. And don't be surprised if you find there are many such moments. The African Diaspora has had to be resilient and keep going. It's why there are so many Negro Spirituals. Don't look at all of them as mournful dirges, but as songs of resistance and freedom and joy. Many of them were coded to be exactly that for slaves committed to freedom on their own terms. And in that complete picture, we do have cause for celebration and pride in who we are and where we come from. Your family has a rich heritage, and if they don't already know it, it's up to you to discover and share it with them!

On the flip side, you also can't allow the tough parts to fill you with rage (which is few steps past angry), or bitterness (which is a few steps past rage). Frustration and even anger with the past is okay. When you find your ancestor's manumission papers, a range of emotions may go through you. Seeing with your own eyes the document that states how much your ancestor had to pay someone for their or their child's freedom might put you in a difficult headspace. All of that is perfectly normal and okay. Let yourself feel all the feels. What is not okay is using the past or even the present as an excuse to not do your best and be your best. Let your anger motivate you to do something. and be a positive force for change. People who allow themselves to wallow in the sins of the past or the present aren't doing themselves or anyone else any good.

So what do we do with all this…stuff? Well, first, know that it's okay not to always be okay. Acknowledge the hurt and the pain. But remember that your ancestors went through all that so that your future could be brighter than theirs ever would or could. Say a prayer for those who have passed, or even have a ceremony for your deceased ancestors as a way to honor their sacrifice. Use the past to both contextualize your present and act as a springboard for you to reclaim your own narrative. for your future. Okay, that sounded kind of college textbook-y. Sorry :)

Use all that passion and energy to focus on restorative justice, either within yourself, your family or the larger community. Restorative justice is actually an African concept known as ubuntu or "humanity". In a genealogical context, as you do the research on your family history, you are restoring the voices of your ancestors. Sometimes all it takes is acknowledging the past and what has happened, and then coming up with a gameplan to move forward in a healthy way. Maybe it's choosing an ancestor's birthday to pour libation and say a prayer. Maybe it's being brave and having hard conversations with your friends of different ethnicities about what a reconciliation with the past really means. That it's not about blaming the living for the sins of the dead, but about acknowledging the systems that got us to where we are, and being willing to find solutions that create greater equity.

Then, focus on the concept of reparative genealogy. This can also be about paying it forward—with random acts of kindness or in a more structured and genealogical way. Making your family records available to others is an act of resistance and an act of justice at the same time. Reconciliation and healing can only come through acknowledging that you are hurting. Maybe it's from something that happened yesterday or maybe it's a case of post-traumatic slave syndrome[4]—a documented mental health phenomenon. We all have to find healthy ways to cope with pain and trauma. If nothing else, take comfort in the fact that you are here and it's not by accident (no matter what anyone else says). Take comfort in the strength and resilience of your ancestors from generations past. Let that be your first step towards healing.

A Note on Mental Health

It's only recently (compared to other groups) that mental health has become an open topic for discussion in African American communities and families. As more and more Black people in the public eye address their own mental wellness, it has become easier for many of us to open up as well. Still, in many Black families, it can be hard to talk about the hard things. But you have to know that you are not alone. Use your family history to build yourself up. And if you can't turn up anything but a line of crooks and rogues, well, hey at least you'll have some really interesting stories to tell, right? But seriously, if you can't find anyone to look to for inspiration in your own family, take comfort in the greater Pan-African fam.

We are all in this together. In fact…

There are so many of us out here doing amazing things. Find someone that resonates with who you are and who you want to be, and let them motivate you to show up every day, and be your best self.

Who knows, maybe one day you'll be just like Joyner Lucas. Lucas wrote a song called "Will" which was a tribute to Will Smith whom he'd looked up to his entire life. Will saw the video (which is amazing) and they met and did a remix (which is even more amazing).

Album cover for Will the Remix

Seven Rules For A Resilient Life

1. Make peace with your past so it won't screw up your present.

2. What others think of you is none of your business.

3. Time heals almost everything. Give it time.

4. Don't compare your life to others, and don't judge them. You have no idea what their journey is all about.

5. Stop thinking too much, it's alright not to know all the answers. They will come to you when you least expect it.

6. No one is in charge of your happiness except you.

7. Smile. You don't own all the problems in the world.

---

1. www.reparations4slavery.com/reparative-genealogy/
2. Based on natural evolutionary relationship.
3. Nia West-Bey, "Young Minds Matter: Historical and Cultural Trauma," 2019
4. PTSS is shorthand for the complex matrix of cognitions, thoughts, and emotions that exist within the African American community, or even Black communities throughout the Diaspora that are rooted in slavery, or the oppressive history that the Black communities have experienced over time.

Chapter 16

Starting Your Family History Search

Okay, now that we've gotten all that out of the way, let's look at how you can start doing genealogy for yourself and your family. We aren't going to go super deep because this is a beginner handbook. But we want to give you enough to get started.

Rule number one: Have fun with it!

Rule number two: Whatever happens, refer to rule number one!

Four our intent and purpose, we are defining genealogy as the study of family history. We are doing the basic research (who, what, when, where) but we are also going beyond and really digging into family lore. And whatever nuggets we find buried in the family history will be brought to the light of day and examined against other sources to verify their accuracy. It's been around for as long as people have been on the planet. Genealogy is the thing that connects you to your past—both the people and the places. When you know where you come from, it grounds you and helps you to understand yourself better. Why do you only like green grapes and not red ones? Why are you so good at coding, or learning languages? Is that short thumb hereditary? So. Many. Questions. You are a unique combination of the people who came before you. Wouldn't you like to get to know them a little better? Are you wondering how—and when?

I'm glad you asked! As for when, now is as good a time as any! It doesn't take anything special to get started with your family genealogy except a willingness to be curious, talk to family members, and eventually, spend some time in libraries, churches, courthouses, and anywhere else the records search takes you.

1. Start with yourself: Complete a pedigree chart (family tree) for yourself and family group record for your family.

2. Write your own life story. This can be an important exercise as it may show you where the gaps are in your knowledge of some events—like how your first day of kindergarten went.

3. Carefully record your family stories. While they may not be completely factual, they will contain a good amount of useful information that can get you started on your research. Don't assume you already know everything you need to know about your parents. Ask them plenty of questions too. And then do the same with your aunts and uncles.

4. Uncover your family health history. Many diseases are genetic, so it's important to know what may run in your family.

5. If possible, go visit the places your ancestors lived. There may not be any building there anymore, but if you can, just stand in the places your ancestors stood and think about their lives. Use all of your senses to imagine the long-ago environment.

6. Collect recipes from your older relatives. Many of those recipes have been handed down through generations. Discover the backstory.

7. Visit a cemetery where your ancestors are buried. If you don't live close to where your ancestors are buried, locate a Black cemetery in your hometown and plan a trip there. When you go, think about what their lives must have been like. If you live in a rural area, it is possible that the cemetery will be next to a Black church.

8. Plan a family reunion. Ask other relatives to help. You could design a t-shirt with the family surnames. Set up some oral interviews and talk to people there.

9. Search your home for clues. You know there are a stack of old photo albums at Granny's house. These and old scrapbooks are treasure troves of

information. Search your home for family memorabilia such as, vital records (birth certificates), family bibles, old letters and diaries, high school yearbooks, fraternity memberships, travel memorabilia, and more. Each has a story to tell about family members.

10. Interview relatives, especially the elderly. Auntie Jewel and Uncle Jerome may have the wildest stories about Los Angeles in the 1980s. Bring out the old photo albums and page through them while you capture their stories on your phone.

We cannot stress enough how important it is for you to start with yourself and your immediate family. This is the foundation for everything else you will uncover.

Charts and appendices are included at the end for you to use as a reference point to record/transcribe some of the information you find. Of course, at some point you'll want to transfer all the information you collect to a program online. There are several free sites for you to do that. You'll find information about that in here too.

Once you get really serious about genealogy—and you will because how could you not find all of this utterly and totally fascinating??—make sure you spend time studying genealogical methods before you start searching sources (whether online, in an archive, or a genealogical library). You want to do this for several reasons. For one thing, if you just start willy-nilly into looking up sources, you are bound to get confused, frustrated, and may even give up. We don't want that!

For example, many beginners of all ages focus on their last name and try to trace that name back to when it first appeared in the United States. This is a mistake for the Black beginner because of the unique circumstances surrounding our arrival to this country. By now, I hope you've grasped the importance of knowing Black history. We know that Black history can be difficult to study because it is often seen as oppressive due to the long shadow of slavery. And no doubt, 400 years casts a pretty long shadow.

In terms of our last names, that can be problematic for many reasons. Most slaves took the name of whomever their owner was when slavery ended in 1865 (or 1867 if you lived in some parts of Texas). But they had the choice of using any name they wanted. Some newly freed people came up with brand new names that held no prior association for them. That was kind of the point—a fresh beginning.

For example, some decided their last name would be Lincoln in honor of the man who emancipated them. So if you are doing a search by last name, that name may not even belong to the family who enslaved your ancestors. And as Black genealogists, we need the names of those slaveowners in order to try to track down verifiable records about our ancestors. That is our reality.

Reconstruction, the period immediately following the Civil War, gave rise to the Freedmen's Bureau. For many years, those records were difficult to search because they were not digitized and indexed. However, that has changed. All of the records are online (and available for free), and many are indexed.

But let's complicate this a little more (because why not?) Even once slavery ended, Black people still had to deal with racism and discrimination in the form of Jim Crow laws. Those were laws that segregated every aspect of African American life. North and South, Blacks lived in designated neighborhoods, went to segregated schools, worshipped in separate churches, and were buried in separate cemeteries.

The separation didn't stop there. Even government records were kept separate. Sometimes, records were actually filed by race, and some records for a city or county's Black population were kept in the back of the book. There were also Black people who were light enough to pass for white—and many did so. So their records may be in the main part of the book and not in the back. These are challenges you have to know about as you begin your formal research.

We said all that to say that you have to be prepared to approach genealogy with a little bit of a different mindset than Americans of other ethnicities

precisely because of those realities of our Black history. It may go without saying, but, well, yeah, this is also why it's critical to know Black history.

When it comes to genealogy, no single piece of paper (evidence) proves anything. It only offers information and maybe clues for further research. You have to track down as many verified and validated sources as you can (or at least three). And you can only do that if:

1. You know what to look for.

2. You know where to find it.

3. You know how to interpret what you find.

And you can only learn those things through studying the methodology of genealogy. We're not saying you have to spend months and years studying this (although of course we'd be thrilled if you did!), but you really do have to understand how to read and interpret the sources that you find. There are many genealogy classes that you can take that facilitate this learning as well. And you can find a lot of those (free) classes at your local library or genealogy society, or via online webinars or even YouTube.

Don't be intimidated when you go to your local genealogical society, no matter what group is running it. I know it may seem a little overwhelming, but most if not all the members will be thrilled to see you and very happy to help you. And if you do encounter people who are not nice or helpful, that is their personal issue and has nothing to do with you. See if you can get someone else to help you—even if you have to come back another day.

Once you have the basics under your belt, then you are ready to…search local sources. I hate to be the one to have to tell you this: not everything is online. But that's okay. This will give you a reason to go check out the local library, archives, or historical center or genealogical society in your town. Don't discount them— community, city, county, and state histories can provide a great deal of information about what life was like in earlier times. That kind of context is like gold for the genealogist and will very likely provide clues to further your research. As Black family history detectives, we are going to have to get really creative in thinking of places we can search for clues to our pasts.

Chapter 17

What Now? Activities, of course!

At this point, you may be asking yourself, well, what can I do with all this stuff I've collected? So. Many. Things.

As we've said already, we really want you to be your authentic creative self and have fun with genealogy. So we've created a list of cool things you can do on those days when you're feeling creative (and you're also stuck in the house).

#1 Re-create An Ancestor Photo

> How is this family history?
>
> Putting yourself in your ancestor's shoes is a great way to try to understand what their life may have been like.

What to Do and How To Do It:

Find a photograph of someone in your family that is doing something that is easy to recreate. Try to find a similar outfit and then take a picture of yourself in the same pose as your ancestor. Then match up the original photo with the one you made and take a picture.

#2 Create a Photo Collage

What To Do

Make a generation photo collage.

How To Do It

Step 1:

Find pictures of you and your ancestors. If possible, try to find pictures of when you are a similar age or even the same pose.

Step 2:

Put the pictures in chronological order, starting with the oldest one first and ending with the picture of you.

Step 3:

Once the pictures are lined up in a row take a picture of them or scan them to make your generational photo collage.

Step 4:

Print, frame, or post your collage.

#3 Make a Home Movie

How is this family history?

Home movies offer an exceptional way of preserving the past unlike any other medium. Seeing who we were, what we looked like, how we talked, how we acted, and then realizing how we've grown or changed can provide a powerful perspective into our personal and families' lives. Make sure you upload the footage to the cloud or an external hard drive so that if anything happens to your phone or computer, the footage isn't lost.

What To Do

Make a series of home movies of yourself and your family.

How To Do It

Use your video camera (if you actually still have one...), phone, iPad, or another digital recording device to record the following:

1. Film a Day-in-Your-Life

What is your morning routine like? What is your bedtime routine like? What are your sibling and parent's evening routines like? These repetitive series of actions change with time and can be an insightful record of you and your family's typical day. Capturing a daily processor routine can preserve the simple but telling details of your life.

2. Film another family member

A. Ask a parent or sibling if you can spend some time recording them. What do they love to do and why?

B. What does their space in the house look like and why? What do they want you to film and why?

3. Film an Event

Anything goes here. Cookouts. Birthday parties. Basketball games. Recitals. Juneteenth (or any other holiday) celebrations. An event is one of the most common types of footage for home movies. There are big events but there are also small events that are worth documenting. Try filming a family dinner or a family outing. Record a sibling's event.

What other small but significant events take place at your house, neighborhood, or school?

#4 Home Movie Night

How is this family history?

Home movies are a powerful family history record, they can bring out the everyday moments that are small but significant. This medium allows us to see our history in real time. Home movies preserve a visual and verbal record of those we love for not only ourselves but for future generations.

What to Do

Get your family together for a Home Movie Night.

How To Do It

Step 1:

Set a date and invite your family to join you for a special movie night.

Step 2:

On the day of your screening pull out your home movies and make some snacks. Take turns watching your favorite home movies.

Step 3:

Observe what happens as you watch these movies together.

Consider the following:

After watching these films how do you think your family changed over time?

In what ways is life the same? In what ways is life different?

What were your family's responses to the films?

What parts of everyday life could you capture now?

Don't have any home movies? Make some! Recently filmed videos can be fun and interesting to watch too.

#5 Learn A Family Recipe

How is this family history?

The power of cooking is that it keeps your heritage alive at the table. The process of preparing, eating, and cleaning up from a meal allows for conversations, connections, and a chance to be together. Eating together is an important part of creating a strong and healthy family. It also allows space to share and de-stress from the day.

By learning a family recipe, you are also carrying on a tradition. You're learning from the past, continuing the act in the present, and creating the ability to pass your knowledge onto the future.

What to Do and How To Do It

Step 1: Pick a favorite family recipe you recipe you want to cook.

(If you don't know of any existing family recipes then learn how to make your favorite meal growing up or a dish you want to incorporate with your current family cuisine.)

Step 2: Ask the relative who normally cooks it to teach you how to make it. If this isn't possible then try cooking it with another family member.

Step 3: Take a picture of the recipe you chose along with the final product you made. If it's a tricky recipe then you may want to take pictures of, or record the cooking process as well to document how to make it in the future.

Step 4: Eat and enjoy! And maybe share with family :)

#6 Make a Digital Family Museum

How is this family history?

Historical objects turn the past into a physical reality. By touching objects that our ancestors used and learning their stories we can connect with those who used and treasured the keepsake. Take time to really think about the object and how your family member feels or felt when they first obtained it. Ask about any hard times that the object saw them through. You never know what kinds of stories are attached to objects like a favorite shirt.

So it is important to document the stories behind family objects so that their significance can be remembered and passed down to future generations. Without a record of your family heirlooms, they often lose their personal value and are thrown out.

What To Do

Take pictures and gather stories about your family heirlooms.

How To Do It

Step 1:

Start with your parents and ask them what family heirlooms or keepsakes they have. Next, talk with your extended family to see what keepsakes they have. Here are some possible categories to ask them about:

Photographs

Letters

Jewelry

Birth, Death, Marriage Certificates

Newspaper Articles

War Mementos

Furniture

Quilts

Silverware

China

Baby books

Family histories

Family papers

Bibles

Collectibles

Travel mementos

Step 2:

Take a picture of each individual heirloom.

Step 3:

Write down any history about the keepsakes. Make sure you ask if family members can identify people in photographs if their names are not already on the backs of the photos.

Ask questions such as:

Who originally owned this? When did they own it?

Who passed it down to you?

What stories do you know about it?

Step 4:

Compile your pictures, facts, and stories into one document.

Step 5:

Share this document with your family. Chances are that many of them don't know about the existence of their family heirlooms and will be interested to know their stories.

What if your family doesn't have any real keepsakes? Don't worry. Mine didn't. But everyone has something special that they hang onto year in and year out. It may be large or small. I saw a program on PBS about Haiti and a woman was talking about how when she was a child, her mother would send her out every day to take coffee to her father in the sugarcane fields. She loved going—carefully taking the hot coffee to her father was an important job and she'd been entrusted with it. When the coffee was safely delivered, her father would cut her some pieces of sugarcane to eat on the way home. It became their daily ritual. And she associated that coffeepot with the happy memories of her childhood. It held meaning and memory for her. Talk with your parents and grandparents and ask them the stories behind their most prized possessions—no matter their actual "cost". What do they want to pass onto their kids and why?

What about you? What are your most treasured possessions and why? List them here.

#7 Make a Virtual Tour of Your House (Please do not post it on social media)

> How is this family history?
>
> Having a visual record of the place we were raised will provide interesting insights for future generations. These pictures will also help spark memories and stories of the time you spent in these spaces. Especially if your family moves to a different town or country for a parent's job. The home we live in, the room where we sleep, and the places where we spend our time will probably change over the years. By documenting these spaces, you are creating a personal record as well as record for the future.

What To Do

Take pictures or video of the inside and outside of where you live.

How To Do It

Step 1:

Start with the outside of your residence. Walk around your home and capture what it looks like. What does the street you live on look like? What does your yard, balcony, or outside area look like? What does your home look like from the street?

Step 2:

Go inside and take pictures or video of each room in your home. Visually capture a variety of angles, for each room try to get what they call an establishing shot, which means a picture of the entire room, and then close-ups shots of anything specific that you want to showcase.

Step 3:

Compile the pictures or video together in one document or video and upload it to the cloud or an external hard drive if it is a video.

*It's okay if maybe your house isn't the most photogenic. This is about you establishing where you are from. Use it to motivate you to do well enough to buy a better house when you are an adult.

#8 Make a Digital Timeline

How is this family history?

This activity is a great way of reflecting on the achievements and milestones of your life thus far, and also allows you to leave a record for future generations.

What To Do

Make a Digital Timeline of Your Life

How To Do It

Step 1:

Think back on your life and brainstorm at least ten memorable milestones, moments, or achievements. Start with your birth and try your best to remember specific years and dates for each memorable event.

Step 2:

Create a new blank image using a digital drawing tool like MS Paint, GoogleDrawings, Pixlr, Adobe Illustrator, or Photoshop.

Step 3:

Use a line tool to draw a long horizontal line, and then use the same tool to add smaller vertical lines to intersect your timeline - one for each life event you are going to add.

Step 4:

Use a text tool to label each vertical line with a date and a short description of the event.

Step 5:

Add pictures to illustrate each event on your time-line. You can use digital photos already saved on your computer, scan in hard copies of photos, or just use Google Image Search to find generic photos and clipart that match each of your events.

Step 6:

Save your timeline to your computer or the cloud. Print a hard copy and save it in a journal or memory box.

Additional Resources

pixlr.com

Google Drawings

Note: It would be easy to do a paper-version of this timeline activity! Just get big pieces of white paper, markers or colored pencils, and rulers to draw straight lines. You could hand-illustrate it or glue on any printed photos you might have.

#9 Write Your Autobiography

> How is this family history?
>
> Writing an autobiography is a valuable way to record your current perspective, philosophies, and goals. Stories that are vivid and clear to you right now might fade away with time. By recording your thoughts and memories they will be available to you and others as the years go by. One day this will likely be a treasured piece of family history for you and your family.

What To Do

Write an autobiography about your life.

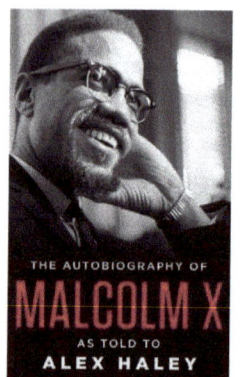

How To Do It

Step 1:

Pick out a cover for your Autobiography or create your own:

Step 2:

Find an autobiography template online or create your own. These types of templates have questions and fun facts for you to fill out about your life. If you prefer you can also add your own questions too.

Step 3:

Fill out the questions from the template.

Step 4:

Print out your autobiography and attach the cover.

Step 5:

Put it in a special place.

#10 Make a podcast. For example, this could be the topic:

How is this family history?

Names are an important part of family history. When doing research using family names can be crucial to finding the right relatives. Peoples' names can be a part of their story.

Why that name?

Make a podcast about you and your family members' names.

How To Do It

Step 1:

Use your phone, computer, tablet, or any other device that has a digital recorder.

Step 2:

Interview and record your family members about their name. Consider asking questions like:

What is your full name?

Where did your name come from?

Were you named after anyone or anything?

What do you like about your name?

What do you not like about your name?

If you could choose another name, what would it be?

Has your name impacted you an any way for good or bad?

Are there any funny stories relating to your name?

Ask your parents how they chose your name.

Ask your parents how they chose your siblings' names.

Step 3:

Throughout your interviews notate what thoughts and discoveries you have. If you want to, incorporate these notes into your podcast then record yourself talking through your thoughts or reading your notes.

Step 4:

Put the digital files of each interview together to create one complete audio file. If you want, add your recorded thoughts at the beginning, in between or after the interviews to add insight or explanation.

Step 5:

Name and export your audio file.

Step 6:

Make a digital copy of it.

Step 7:

Share your podcast with your family!

Consider the following:

Did you learn anything new about your name?

Did you learn anything new about your family member's name?

Does it make you think any differently about the importance of a name?

#11 Make A Documentary About A Family Tradition

How is this family history?

Traditions are an extremely important part of a family. By recording your family tradition, you are showing interest and support in your family and their traditions. You are preserving an important aspect of your family history and the film will provide fun and interesting insights to you as you get older.

What To Do

Film a family tradition

How To Do It

Step 1. Pick a family tradition

It can be a big tradition like taking an annual family vacation to the beach or a smaller one like flying the Pan-African flag from your front porch and hosting a family cookout in honor of Juneteenth.

Step 2. Film the process

Use your video camera, phone, iPad, or another recording device. Don't just film the event itself; film the setup, take down, and everything that happens in between. For example, if your family makes a red velvet cake for Christmas every year, film them making the cake, decorating the cake, and eating it. This way you capture the small but important moments that happen along the way.

Step 3. Show the film

Sit down with your family and enjoy the film. Burn it to a DVD or upload it to a private site, external hard drive, or the cloud to make sure it is saved.

#12 Make A Time Capsule

How is this family history?

Physical objects help the hazy past turn into a tactile reality. The objects you place in your time capsule will spark stories, memories, and thoughts from your life.

What To Do

Gather photos, letters, and meaningful objects to make a time capsule.

How To Do It

Step 1: Decide who your audience is.

Who do you want to open this time capsule? You? Your kids? Your grandkids? Your intended audience will determine what you include in your capsule.

Step 2: Gather items such as:

- A letter to your future self about what you think you do, where you think you will live, and what you have hoped you have done

- A screenshot of the front page of your local newspaper today

- A record or mixtape

- Photos: a picture of you doing something meaningful, or of your family

- A coin or form of currency from this year

- A list of goals you want to achieve by the time you open the capsule

- A piece of clothing or jewelry. (In case this does become forgotten over time don't include anything too valuable or irreplaceable.)

- A piece of current technology - again, nothing irreplaceable.

- A handwritten letter from your parent or grandparent to your future self

Step 3: Choose a durable container

Choose a container that will last the longest in your chosen hiding spot. Metal cans or a sturdy shoebox work really well. Fill your container and seal it with duct tape.

Step 4: Mark on the time capsule the date you want it opened.

Step 5: Store your time capsule in a safe and secret place.

Step 6: Don't forget about it!

#13 Send a Letter to Your Future Self

How is this family history?

By writing a letter to your future self you are looking ahead, setting a path you want to follow, and creating a physical copy of a road map in which you can look back to see how you did.

What To Do

Write a letter to your future self.

How To Do It

Step 1:

Pull out your computer or some pen and paper.

Step 2:

Pick a time in your future you want to write to. Here are a few ideas:

A. 1, 5, 10, or 25 years from now

B. When you graduate from high school

C. When you graduate from college

D. When you buy your first house

E. When you have your first child

F. When you turn a certain age

Step 3:

Write a letter to yourself answering questions such as these:

Where do you predict you will be at this time?

What do you predict you will be doing in your work, school, and family life?

In what ways do you hope you will be the same?

In what ways do you hope you will be different?

What do you want to learn from now until then?

What advice do you have for your future self?

What family and friends do you hope you are still close to?

What do you want to do with your life from now until then?

What goals do you want to accomplish from now until then?

My greatest example is _____. I hope I can become like them in the following ways....(list them here)

Ask yourself, "Do you still....?"

I hope I never......

I hope I always....

Step 4:

Handwritten letters: Seal your letter in an envelope, address it to yourself, and mark the date it should be opened.   Put it with your important documents like birth certificate or passport so you don't lose it.

Electronic Letters: Go to futureme.org. Copy and paste your letter into the text box and enter in the date you want your letter emailed to you. On the date you chose futureme.org will email you your letter. It is private so it will be sent only to your email. Make sure you keep your email updated on the site!

Step 5:

When the future date comes, read it!

#14 Make Your Family Health Tree

How Is This Family History?

Many health issues are genetically related. Knowing your family's health history will better prepare you to know what health issues to look for, be checked for, and to be aware of. In case of an emergency, having a document like this could help doctors and medical professionals better diagnose and treat a health issue, too.

And given the disparity in healthcare for Black and brown communities, a document like this may help save a life.

Does this sound weird? It could save a life one day!

What To Do

Make your family's health tree

How To Do It

Step 1:

Start with you and your immediate family. Write down what allergies, blood type, and health issues each family member has. Find out the answers to questions like:

What blood type are you? What allergies do you have?

Do you have any chronic conditions, such as heart disease, diabetes, asthma, or high blood pressure?

Has anyone in the family had birth defects, learning problems, or developmental

disabilities, such as Down's syndrome?

Have you had any major surgeries? If so, what for?

Have you had cancer? If so, what type?

Have you struggled with any addictions?

What other health issues have you experienced?

Step 2:

Contact your aunts, uncles, and grandparents. Let them know you are collecting information about your family's health history. Ask them the same questions as above.

Find out what illnesses their late parents or grandparents had. How old were they when they died? What caused their deaths?

Step 3:

Collect the information you've gathered and put it into one document.

Step 4:

Print it out and put it with your other important documents such as your birth certificate.

Step 5:

Give a copy of the health history to your doctor and family members.

Unless you have permission, do not share anyone else's health information.

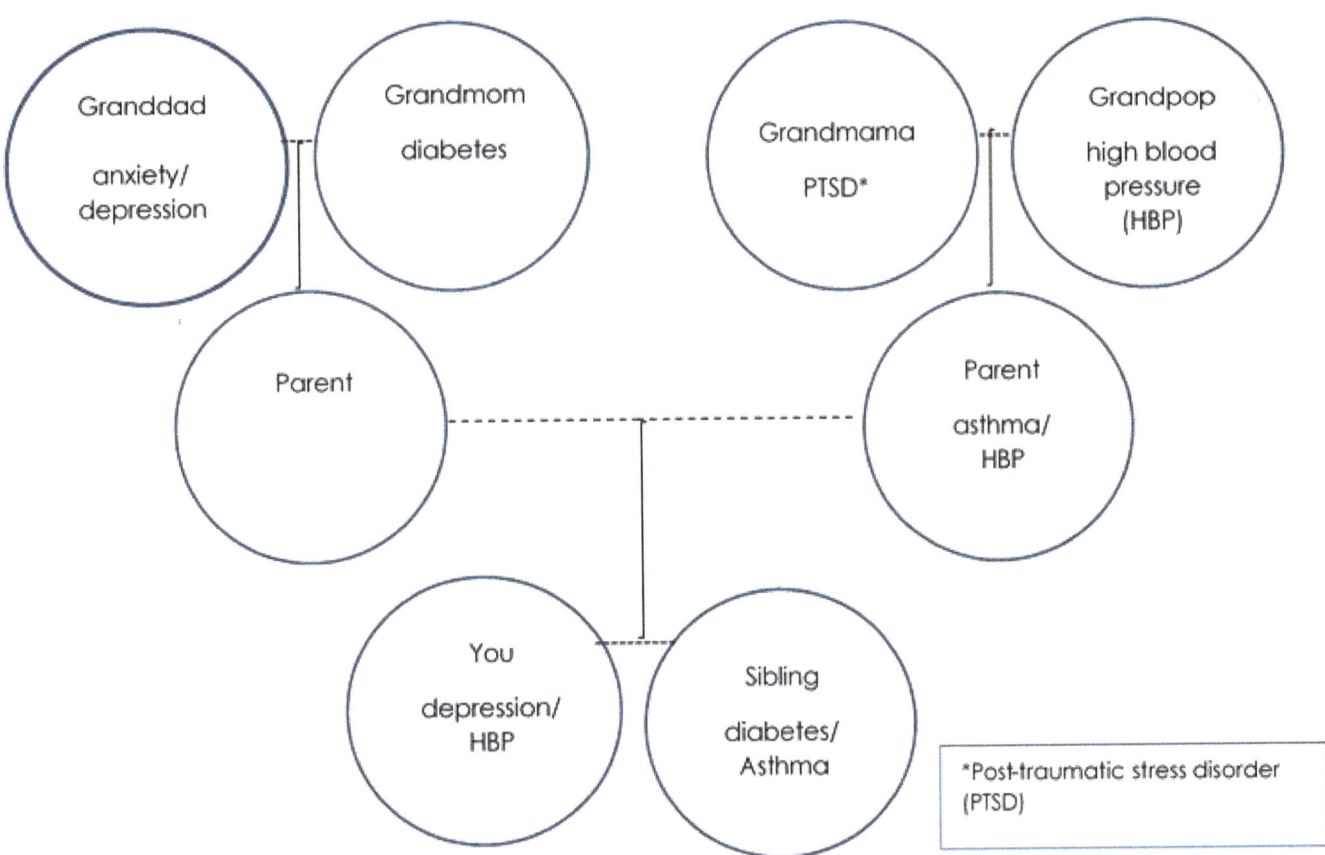

Additional Resources:

This is a free online template to create your family health tree. It will also help you learn about your risk for conditions that can run in families: https://familyhistory.hhs.gov/FHH/html/index.html

You can document your family health history here: Tapgenes.com

For more questions that you can ask your family members about their health, check out:

https//www.cdc.gov/Features/FamilyHealthHistory

https://nihseniorhealth.gov/creatingafamilyhealthhistory/faq/faq9.html

#15 Make An Audio Documentary

(Yes, you can call it a podcast if you want)

> ### How Is This Family History?
>
> Audio documentaries are like home movies but highlight different aspects. People's voices come to the fore. It's really special to listen to someone's voice. Someday you may be far from your loved one and you can listen to their voice that you treasure. People also may be more relaxed around an audio recorder; they may be more likely to forget it's there.

What To Do

Make an audio documentary about your family

How To Do It

Step 1:

Use the recording feature on your phone or iPad.

Step 2:

Pick a person or a family activity you would like to document.

Some ideas are:

·   A birthday: think of the preparation of making the cake, lighting the candles, blowing them out

·   Your mom, dad, or sibling as they're doing a chore around the house

·   A conversation with your parents

·   A trip to the store with a family member

The idea of an audio documentary is a little different than recording an interview with a family member. In an audio documentary you want to do more than ask questions and record answers. It's like making a home movie, you want to record as events unfold. The reason for focusing on audio is that you capture and focus on different things. Also, people respond differently when you have a voice recorder versus having a camera.

Step 3:

Record your activity. If you're able, aim your microphone at whomever is speaking or where the most action is taking place. Also, try to record 30 seconds to 1 minute of what's called "room tone". Just record the room or space you're in for a bit while nothing is happening, and no one is speaking. This way when you make cuts, you can slip in a little room tone if needed, to break up the things people say and give a natural flow to the finished product.

Step 4:

Upload your file to your hard drive or the cloud. You can use a free software called Audacity, which you can download from the internet, to edit your documentary. (audacityteam.org)

#16 Place [Location] Stories

How is this family history?

Place (location) is also a huge part of knowing who you are, because it is where your family comes from. Or it may just hold a deep meaning for you (that you may or may not be able to explain). Either way, it can inform your identity just as much as members of your family can.

What To Do

Create a Place Story

How To Do It

Step 1:

Think about a meaningful place in your life or in your family history

Step 2:

In your browser, type: https://instantstreetview.com

Step 3:

Take a screenshot of the place, save it to your computer or device, print it out, or click the "share" link.

Step 4:

Write a caption to accompany your screenshot. Explain why this place is important to you.

Step 5:

Share the picture of your place and description with a family member. Ask them about a place that is significant to them.

It may be a small church out in the country. Or it may be Hampton, Virginia, where the first English ship brought Africans in 1619.

You may not understand why any Black person would have wanted to remain in the South after the Civil War. And truth be told, thousands did migrate to other cities in search of better prospects.

But for the ones who stayed, why did they? Sometimes it's not easy to explain a connection to a particular place. William W. Falk's book, Rooted in Place: Family and Belonging in a Southern Black Community follows the lives of a large extended family whose members talk about schooling, relatives, work, religion, race, and their love of the place where they have lived for generations. Falk describes an interconnectedness between race and place in the area that helps explain African Americans' loyalty to it. In addition to Black people being in the majority population-wise, there were deep cultural roots and longstanding webs of social connections that, Falk found, more than outweighed the racism they faced and the economic disadvantages they suffered.

#17 Create a Vision Board

> How Is This Family History?
>
> Having a vision board can help youth (and adults) consciously choose what direction they are heading, goals they want to accomplish, and family traits they want to pass on. This is a creative project to visually see one's goals and help youth realize how they want to make history.

What To Do

Make a vision board that reflects your goals and dreams

How To Do It

Step 1:

Grab markers, scissors, tape, magazines, and a large sheet of paper or posterboard.

Step 2:

Consider the following questions:

What are my educational goals?

What are my career goals?

What are my health goals?

What are my spiritual goals?

What personal talents do I want to develop?

What habits do I want to continue and what habits do I want to break?

What family traits and habits do I want to embrace and pass on?

What family traditions and habits do I not want to pass on?

Step 3:

Cut or print out visuals that reflect your goals. Paste these pictures onto your poster board. Add illustrations and words to your pictures that describe your goals.

Step 4:

Hang your board somewhere you can see it often.

Step 5:

Make occasional updates to your vision board. Over time some of your goals may change. You will probably discover new talents you want to develop or hobbies you want to pursue. Update your vision board to reflect who you want to be and where you want to go in life.

#18 StoryCorps App

> How is this family history?
>
> Recording first person stories is one of the best ways to document history. With this free app kids of all ages can participate in making history just by using their phones.

What To Do

Interview a family member using the free StoryCorps app.

How To Do It

Download the free app at https://storeycorps.me/

Choose a relative or close friend you want to interview. Pick from the list of questions provided in the app, use the questions in this handbook, or come up with your own questions and stories you want to record. Find a quiet place to conduct your interview. Listen carefully as you record your story and be curious. Once your interview is done you have the option of uploading it into the Library of Congress, sharing it with others, or just saving it for your own family.

How To Do It

Go to storycorps.me to download the free app. Choose a relative or close friend you want to interview. Pick from the list of questions provided in the app, use the questions in this handbook, or come up with your own questions and stories you want to record. Find a quiet place to conduct your interview. Listen carefully as you record your story and be curious. Once your interview is done you have the option of uploading it into the Library of Congress, sharing it with others, or just saving it for your own family.

Additional Resources:

To watch more animated interviews, check out the StoryCorps YouTube Channel.

Chapter 18

Family Interviews

Get After Those Family Interviews!

Interviewing your immediate and extended family members is very important to the Black genealogist. You'll be amazed at what you can learn from older members of your family. It won't always be rainbows and sunshine, but even hearing about the hard stuff can be rewarding. Because it will give you a better understanding of your heritage as well as the challenges and the accomplishments of different relatives. The memories you gather can be collected not just or yourself, but for future generations of your family.

1.   Make a list of people you want to interview. How are you related to them?

2.   Will this be a group interview or an individual interview? There are pros and cons to each method. In group interviews, it's possible that what one person says will jog the memory of someone else and you get fuller, richer stories. In an individual interview, you can ask targeted questions that really get at the core of who that person is.

3.   Will you meet in person, on the phone, or via an online video platform—i.e., Facetime, Skype, Facebook, Microsoft teams, etc.

4.   Think through what it is you really want to learn about. And if you aren't really sure, that's okay. Think of your interviews as fact-gathering missions.

5.   Ask around and see if one of your older relatives has created a family tree or collected genealogical information for your family. That way, you can just continue the work that has already been started.

The Particulars

1. Create a list of questions for each family member (see next page). You could have a standard list, or you could customize

it for each person. For example, if you know that your grandmother served in the Navy, make sure to include questions about her military service. Ask open-ended questions that allow them space to tell stories.

2. Make sure you schedule a time that is convenient for them—especially if you live in a different time zone! BE VERY CLEAR about time zones!

3. Send the questions in advance so the family member has time to recall their past. And if you don't really know the family member well, it's a good way to connect with them.

4. Are you going to record your phone conversation or video meeting? Be sure to ask their permission first as it can be illegal to record without consent.

5. Don't forget to ask about artifacts and memorabilia (family Bible, high school, and college yearbook, etc.) and photographs from the past. A lot of people still have boxes of old photos around the house. Ask if they can bring them to the meeting and talk about the photos. Then see if they will allow you to either have the photos or make copies.

6. Official documents like a birth certificate, marriage license, a DD214 (for members of the military), etc., are great primary sources. Collect and make copies of these items.

7. Other documents like a newspaper article or an obituary, are great sources of information too!

8. Remember that for many decades, the church (regardless of the denomination) was a very important part of most Black people's lives. So don't forget to stop by your family church and talk to the secretary to see if there might be church records you can analyze. Most churches will have annual lists of their members, and many create anniversary books that showcase various members as well. Church records, especially from the 1930s - 1990s are a treasure for Black genealogists.

Expert Tip: Break up your interview questions into sections:

Childhood (Age 0-10)

School age (11-19)

Young Adult (20-30)

Adult (31-50)

Middle age (51-75)

Elderly (76+)

We think some of the best questions are the personal ones – the kind that may be slightly embarrassing or may make the narrator laugh or cry. These are the questions no one ever has the nerve to ask, and the answers to which you won't find recorded anywhere. Obviously, you don't want to start the interview with a question like "So whatever happened to crazy Uncle Joe?" or, "Tell me about Cousin Ike's five-year bid." But once you're about hallway through, or even nearly finished, and the subject is comfortable with you, go ahead and ask. But do it delicately. The last thing you want is to upset anyone. You might even preface your question with, "You don't have to answer this if you don't want to, but it is part of our family story, so can you talk about…..?".

Sample Oral Interview Questions

1. Am I named after a family member? Who, and why?

2. What holiday/traditions did my grandparents celebrate as a child?

3. What sorts of health issues run in our family?

4. What do "Day of the Dead" celebrations look like in our family?

5. Is the way I'm being raised different from how my dad was raised?

6. Does my family have a history of social justice activism?

7. How did the LA race riot affect my father in 1992?

8. What types of things/events did my great-grandfather have to endure in Iowa—being one of only a few Black people in his area?

9. What was it like being an Afro-Peruvian woman in Chincha?

10. What was it like for the early generations of my family asBlack settlers in Canada's Yukon territory?

11. How did my relative's participation Desert Shield/Desert Storm impact my family and what does that mean to me today?

12. What is the originof the surname on my maternal side?

13. Why did my family emigrate from Panama to Wyoming?

14. How did the Vietnam War affect children during the 1950s and until the end of the war?

15. What was life like for my mom growing up as an Afro-Cuban woman in Havana?

16. How did my granddaddy lose his leg? Was it health-related?

17. Did anyone in our family ever start a business? What happened to it?

18. Was anyone in our family ever the victim of violence? What happened?

19. Why did my grandmama's family choose to move to Chicago from Mississippi during the Great Migration?

20. What was it like for great-grandaddy to live in New York City when Black people had more opportunity but still weren't treated equally?

21. There is a tradition to pass a family name down from father to son in each generation. How far back does that go?

22. What was it like to travel during your childhood? Did your family have a "green book"?

23. What was it like for great-grandmama and her family to live in the segregated South?

24. Did anyone in our family write poetry?

Chapter 19

Give Back To Your Community!

<u>Black Cemeteries</u>

There is a very, very, very good chance that your city or town has a Black cemetery. It may be on the grounds of a church or in a forgotten corner of the

city. Black cemeteries tend not to be as well maintained, even when they are owned by the city. Additionally, the members of most churches are elderly and unable to properly care for the final resting place of their loved ones. They would welcome your help. Go online and find out where the cemetery is, take your siblings or friends, and plan to spend some time picking up trash, cleaning headstones, and weeding. Martin Luther King Jr. Day (the third Monday in January) is traditionally a day of service.

Other good dates might be September 27 which is Ancestor Appreciation Day—a holiday devoted to the celebration of diversity and cultural heritage. November 1- 2, also known as the Day of the Dead in Latin America, is also a great time to do this. November 2 especially, as it is known as All Soul's Day, when people are encouraged to pray for the souls of family and friends. As you work, think about the lives of the people who are buried in the cemetery, as well as your own ancestors. Try not to focus on the hardships of our people, but their deep sense of joy and spirituality. That is the legacy they leave us.

<u>HBCUs, Black Genealogical Societies, and Church Archives</u>

If you live in a town with a historically Black college or university (HBCU), you're in luck. Those can be goldmines for the genealogist. But they often have very small staff for their archives and records departments. This is also true of many Black genealogical societies, churches, and other Black institutions that have very small or non-existent budgets. Go by and see if you can volunteer to index or digitize records. You have no idea how unbelievably helpful this would be for people who need to view those records, but who may never be able to travel to your city to look up those documents in person.

You should even be able to get credit at your high school or college for this!

Volunteering at Federal Records Repositories

Did you know that you can get involved in fun genealogy-related projects? For example, you can tackle some indexing. Indexing means reading original records and entering the information into a set form so that it is available for searching. This is crucial for making documents easy to find. And of course, you should be able to get credit at your school for your volunteer work. And if you live near one of the National Archives or Federal Records Centers across the country, in-person volunteer opportunities abound! For remote/digital indexing, you can find more information at: www.archives.gov/citizen-archivist/volunteers

Be a Geo-Tagger

At BillionGraves.com, you can volunteer by using your smartphone to take geo-tag photos of headstones.

Then, you can upload your pics to the BillionGraves website, where they will be transcribed by other volunteers so they can be easily accessed for research online.

Chapter 20

Document Your Sources

Yes, this is a thing. And yes, you have to do it if you want your findings to be taken seriously. And no, it's not hard. Once you get to the point where you are scouring courthouse records or digging through microfilm at your local family history center to locate long lost relatives, you definitely want to write down the name of the newspaper or name of the article, the author, and the date it was written, and the location where you found it for your own records. It is impossible to emphasize enough how fundamental this is. This isn't only true for good genealogy, but for good research in general—no matter the subject.

I cannot overstate how critical it is to start off on the right foot. Whether it's the story your mom tells you on the way to school, a weekend phone discussion with Grandpop, or your dad's baby book. You have to be sure to write down the conversation as well as the day and the person you talked to. For things like baby books, write down who it belongs to, how they came to have it, and anything else you discover about where it came from. Don't worry too much about the format just yet. Yes, there is a standard way to cite every source. But right now, the important thing is that you get into

the habit of documenting your sources as thoroughly as possible. If your dad won't let you have his baby book, ask him if you can make a copy of it or at least take a picture of each page. That way, even if the original gets misplaced, you still have a copy.

Expert Tip:

Avoid abbreviations. Your narrative (family history book) will be much more readable, and there's less chance of misunderstanding and miscommunication.

You may be wondering why you would need to go to the courthouse or the archives or the library in the first place. Well, two reasons: traceability and credibility. If I read your family history (because you made it into a graphic novel that became a runaway bestseller) I may find that we're related. While I may not be able to get in touch with you, I can always go to the same courthouse you went to and locate the records you examined. See how that works? And also, it'll keep you from looking at the same records twice if you keep a record of where you went, what you looked at, and what you found there.

Example: Auntie Irene tells you that your great aunt's second Cousin James was an Army officer who was awarded a purple heart in Desert Storm. Unfortunately, James passed before you were born, and the medal is said to be buried with him. How are you going to find out if he really received a purple heart? It's a wonderful story but do you really want to base a claim like that on what amounts to hearsay? (No disrespect to Auntie Irene of course). And you can't exactly go dig up the casket. For this, you would need to search military records—many of which are online. You may be able to find a record in a free database like Familysearch.com, but you may have to go to a subscriber site like www.fold3.com.

What is a Primary Source?

The short answer is any official document you receive from the government is primary source. Additionally, any document that is a first-hand account is a primary source.

Birth certificates

Marriage licenses

Death certificates

Family Bibles

US census

Wills

Probate records Diaries

Journal

Military records Deeds

Land records

Where Can I Find Primary Sources?

County Clerk's office

County courthouse

National Archives and Records Administration

Library

Online

Family members

What is a Secondary Source?

TNBT (the next best thing). Seriously though, secondary sources aren't any less important, they are just second-hand accounts of something. And yes, I know. It seems like a letter would be a primary source. But it's not.

Some types of secondary sources:

Letters

Newspapers

Obituaries

Family histories

Indexes for census

Collections of cemetery inscriptions

Chapter 21

Citing Sources

There's no getting around it: recording the full citation information from a source right the first time is paramount. No matter how good your memory is, at some point it's all going to blur together, and you won't be able to recall what came from where. It's not enough to say, "Well, I wouldn't have written it down if it weren't true." Whether the source is a probate court record, a yellowed newspaper clipping, auntie's diary, or a conversation with your pops, cite your sources. Whether you take notes on a computer, hand-write them, make copies on a copier or dictate them into a tape recorder, just get into a habit of making thorough notes of where and how you obtained your information. You'll thank yourself later. Most of us (if we're honest) will admit that we've occasionally neglected to do that and had to backtrack -- time and effort we'd rather have spent uncovering new information. Make every effort to note all of the elements of a source while it is still in your hands.

Sources Versus Citations (Whaaat—they' re not the same thing??)

The easiest way to explain this is to say that the source is where you get the information from. It's the book, the person you interviewed, the newspaper article, the birth certificate. Those are all sources. The citation is the way you list all of the information about the source if you use it (the information gleaned from the source) in your family history narrative (your family genealogy book or short film).

Expert Tip:

Be consistent: As a beginner, it's more important that you list all your citations in the exact same format. If, for the first book citation, you list the title first and then the author, do it that way for all of the books you cite.

The Basic Format

Back in the day, we had to go to the library and physically pull books and magazines off shelves. Times have changed, and most information is now pulled from the internet. But some things are still the same, and the basic format for citations looks like this:

BOOK:

Example: Nelson, Aungelic, *For the Culture: A Genealogy Handbook* for the Cool Kids. Panafrigen Press, 2022.

Example for an e-book: Nelson, Aungelic, For the Culture: A Genealogy Handbook for the Cool Kids. E-book ed., Panafrigen Press, 2022.

WEBSITE:

Example: Aungelic Nelson, The Majani Project (www.majani.org: 2022), accessed 22 Feb 22.

ARTICLE (from a website):

Example: Nia West-Bey, "Young Minds Matter: Historical and Cultural Trauma," Hogg Foundation For Mental Health, (https://hogg.utexas.edu/historical-and-cultural-trauma: 8 October 2019), accessed 19 June 2022.

Unpublished Sources

If you are researching your ancestors in a courthouse or in a records repository like the Moorland-Spingarn Research Center at Howard University, you will find documents and records that have never been published. But if you are going to use them as a source, you want to make sure you cite them.

The goal here is to be as specific as you possibly can. Each citation should identify the informant, the place, the date, and the information given, plus to whom it was given and where that information is stored. Comments describing the informant's reliability may be added.

Personal Letter

Sidney Porter, Letter to Imani Porter, 24 December 1960. [The original handwritten letter is in the possession of Imani Porter, Los Angeles, California.]

Oral Interview

Keisha Black Porter and Robert Anthony Black. Oral interview, 22 February 2022, by De'Shawn Black at Keisha's home in St. Louis, Missouri. Digital phone recording and partial transcription in the possession of De'Shawn Black, St. Louis, Missouri.

Photograph

Photograph of the Black Family Reunion,2008, FDR Park, Philadelphia, Pennsylvania. Taken by Antwan Black, June 2008. Copy in possession of Antwon Black, Washington D.C.

Email

Malcolm X, New York, [malcolmx@gmail.com to Martin Luther King Jr., email, 1 January 1963, "Collaboration"; privately held by Elijah Green [EBGreen@aol.com], Atlanta, GA.

Official Records

Vital Records

Death Certificate for James Black, 2 November 2019, File No. 75982, Missouri State Board of Health. Certified copy in possession of Antwan Black.

Certificate of Marriage, Malik King to Jaleesa Carter,19 June 1919, Henrico County, Virginia. Virginia Department of Health, Office of Vital Records, Richmond, Virginia. Copy in possession of Jordan Carter King, Richmond, VA.

Census Record

Most census records these days will be accessed online via a genealogy website like Family Search or Ancestry. The first example is if you make a trip to the National Archives and Records Administration and get a roll of microfilm to sift through. The second example is if you search one of the databases online. Fortunately, they do a good job of listing the citation for you. You only have to copy and paste it to your document.

Example 1: 1850 United State Census (Free Schedule), Pitt Township, Wyandot County, Ohio; p. 233, family 86, dwelling 79, lines 967-977; June 1, 850; National Archives Microfilm M-19, Roll 719.

Example 2: United States Census, 1930," database with images, FamilySearch (https://www.familysea rch.org/ark:/61903/1:1:HNF7-1N2: accessed 7 February 2022), Hugh Masingale, Precinct 3, Panola, Texas, United States; citing enumeration district (ED) ED 11, sheet 3A, line 24, family 46, NARA microfilm publication T626 (Washington D.C.: National Archives and Records Administration, 2002), roll 2382; FHL microfilm 2,342,116.

Legal Records

Deed of Sale from Pearl Morris to Redd Thomas, 14 February 1872 (filed 31 August 1872), Webster County, Missouri, Deed Book D, page 703. County Recorder's Office, Marshfield, Missouri.

Expert Tip:

Be consistent: As a beginner, it's more important that you list all your citations in the exact same format. If, for the first book citation, you list the title first and then the author, do it that way for all of the books you cite.

Chapter 22

Free African American Online Resources

There are a great big bunch of free resources available to the beginning Black genealogist!! Most of these sites provide free accounts where you can

complete a family tree and/or research your family.

The Majani Project

This site is a free online genealogy club for Black and brown youth. Get on the mailing list to learn about upcoming virtual training tips of how to study your family history, hear special guest webinars on various genealogy topics, and take cool workshops. **Majani.org**

Digital Library on American Slavery

This online archive houses records related to the 15 slave states plus Washington, DC, as well as a number of Northern states. You'll find information about more than 100,000 individuals in runaway slave notices, slave deeds, and court petitions, and more. **Dlas.uncg.edu**

AfricaMap

Africamap is housed at the Center for Geographic Analysis at Harvard University with an initial grant from the Harvard Provosts Fund for Innovative Computing and ongoing support from the Hutchins Center, the Department of African and African American Studies, and the Committee for African Studies at Harvard University. **https://worldmap.maps.arc.gis.com/home/item.html**

African American Coal Miners

This site was created for the purpose of sharing over ten years of information collected that relates to African American coal miners. It also provides a vehicle for others with additional information, however small or large, to contribute to this body of knowledge. It is hoped that through this effort, family historians will locate missing ancestors, and researchers will be inspired to conduct serious research and publish materials related to this underdeveloped subject area. **Freepages.rootsweb.com/~Blackcoalm iners/genealogy.index.htm**

African Ancestry

African Ancestry is an Africa-specific DNA testing site. It works to identify the ethnic groups of your ancestors. **Africanancestry.com**

The African American Mosaic

The Library of Congress has published The African-American Mosaic: A Library of Congress Resource Guide for the Study of Black History and Culture. A noteworthy and singular publication, the Mosaic is the first Library-wide resource guide to the institution's African American collections. Covering the nearly 500 years of the black experience in the Western hemisphere, the Mosaic (both the book and the LOC's actual exhibit) surveys the full range size, and variety of the Library's collections, including books, periodicals, prints, photographs, music, film, and recorded sound. **www.loc.gov/exhibits/african**

Afrigeneas

This site was created to assist the Black genealogist with locating data. Information within tax records, diaries, plantation records and data on runaway slaves that may be helpful is indexed by last name, state, and year. In addition to a wealth of how-to tips and message boards, AfriGeneas also offers census records, slave data, an index of 50,168 surnames and a collection of 16,338 death records. **www.afrigeneas.com**

Afro-Louisiana History and Genealogy 1719-1820

The fruits of 15 years of work by Gwendolyn Midlo Hall, this site employs powerful search tools to comb through data on 100,000 Louisiana slaves. **www.ibiblio.org/laslave**

Ancestry.com African American Collection 1719-1820

Ancestry has compiled a treasure trove of information for the Black genealogist. **www.ancestry.co morg/search/categories/aabooks**

Slave Narratives from the Federal Writers Project 1936-1938

Born in Slavery: Slave Narratives from the Federal Writers' Project, 1936-1938 contains more than 2,300 first-person accounts of slavery and 500 black-and-white photographs of former slaves. These narratives were collected in the 1930s as part of the Federal Writers' Project (FWP) of the Works Progress Administration, later renamed Work Projects ministration (WPA). **www.loc.gov/collections/slave -narratives-from-the-federal-writers-project-1936-1938/about-this-collection/**

Christine's African American Genealogy Website

Christine Charity's site is very helpful one for researching African American ancestors. There are links and information about the post-Civil War Freedmen's Bureau records, African genealogy, and related articles and databases. **www.ccharity.com**

Civil War Soldiers and Sailors

Search names and regimental stories of the Union Army's African American units, or link to other National Park sites that interpret Civil War history. **www.nps.gov/civilwar/soldiers-and-sailors-da tabase.htm**

Cyndi's List for African American Genealogy

200-plus African American genealogy links are listed by category. **www.cyndislist.com/african-am erican**

Documenting the American South

A site hosted by the University of North Carolina with collections such as The Church in the Southern Black Community, Colonial and State Records of North Carolina, and North American Slave Narratives. **www.docsouth.unc.edu/neh**

The Encyclopedia Britannica Guide to Black History

Features 600 articles, along with historical film clips and audio recordings, hundreds of photographs and other images, related links and more. **kids.britannica.com/students/articles/African-American-history-timeline/625406**

Enslaved: Peoples of the Historical Slave Trade

A free database containing over 950,000 searchable records of enslaved individuals, slave owners, and others who participated in the slave trade. **Enslaved.org**

Freedmen's Bureau Report

This project was created in partnership with Federal agencies and private organizations on Juneteenth 2015 to develop a searchable online database with nearly 1.8 million records of the formerly enslaved created by the Freedmen's Bureau, which was chartered to help newly emancipated Black men, women, and children after the Civil War. **Discoverfreedmen.org**

International African American Museum Center for Family History

A one-of-a-kind research center for African American genealogists, scheduled to open in 2022. Searchable records include marriage, obituary, Bible records, and more. **Cfh.iiamuseum.org**

African American Historical and Genealogical Society

This nationwide genealogy society also has individual state societies as well. Go online and find the chapter for your state and start attending the meetings. Most of them are all online now. **Aahgs.org**

Free African Americans of the Mid-Atlantic and Upper South

A large site with a lot of information. Two books you can read on-line containing about 2,700 pages of family histories based on all colonial court order and minute books on microfilm at the state archives of Virginia, Maryland, North Carolina, and Delaware (over 1000 volumes), tax lists, wills, deeds, free Negro registers, marriage bonds, parish registers, Revolutionary War pension files, etc. **www.freeafricanamericans.com**

Genealogy Sites for African Ancestries

A "one-stop shop" for many Pan-African sites. You can find sites related to Caribbean genealogy here too. **www.sites.rootsweb.com/~jfuller/gen_mail_african.html**

The Geography of Slavery in Virginia

A digital collection of advertisements for runaway and captured slaves and servants in 18th- and 19th-century Virginia newspapers. **www2.vcdh.virginia.edu/gos/**

Slavery in America and the World: History, Culture & Law

A large legal database with hundreds of books, articles, pamphlets that analyze and discuss slavery from various viewpoints. **home.heinonline.org/content/slavery-in-america-and-the-world/**

Index to Parish Court Slave Emancipation Petitions

Hosted by the City Archives of the New Orleans Public Library, there is a wealth of information available here—including statements of slaves imported into New Orleans. **www.nutrias.org/~nopl/inv/vcp/vcp.htm**

An Index to Freedom Records of Prince George's County

A site managed by the Maryland State Archives, it contains an electronic index of various records. **www.msa.maryland.gov/msa/stagser/s1400/s1411/html/instruct.html**

Lowcountry Africana

African American genealogy in South Carolina, Georgia, and Florida. **www.lowcountryafricana.com**

National Archives' Guide to African American Genealogical Resources

This guide to National Archive records is helpful in finding and researching African American ancestors. There are also links to resources on other sites. **www.archives.gov/research/african-american**

National Archives' Guide to Freedmen's Bureau Records

Guide to NARA's collection of federal records of the Freedmen's Bureau. **www.archives.gov/research/african-american**

Trans-Atlantic Slave Trade Database

A database containing information on thousands of slave voyages made across the Atlantic Ocean. **www.slavevoyages.org**

Texas Slavery Project

This site examines the spread of American slavery into the borderlands between the United States and Mexico from 1820 to 1850. A database has population statistics for slaves and slaveowners. **www.texasslaveryproject.org**

Virginia Slave Names

In 2011, the Virginia Museum of History & Culture launched Unknown No Longer" to make biographical details of enslaved Virginians from unpublished historical records in its collections accessible. **virginiahistory.org/research/collections/unknown-no-longer**

African Americans of the Kentucky Borderlands

A database about African Americans in the Kentucky border region. Information was hidden in plain sight among many primary historic resources, such as church records, brought together here to create one cohesive narrative. **https://omekas.bcplhistory.org/s/borderlands/page/home**

The Lemon Project Genealogy Initiative: Summer Sankofa Series

Sponsored by William & Mary University in Williamsburg, Virginia, this project hosts a free series of genealogy webinars covering topics from family history to genetic genealogy that are also uploaded to YouTube. **www.wm.edu/sites/lemonproject/genealogy/**

BlackProGen LIVE

Organized by eminent genealogist Nicka Sewell-Smith, this is a monthly online gathering of genealogists of all ages and experience levels that get together to discuss genealogy from the perspective of Black people. **BlackProGen LIVE**

Genealogy Adventures Live

A weekly genealogy program on YouTube hosted by Donya Williams and Brian Sheffey with special guests who talk about a variety of genealogy topics. **Genealogy Adventures Live**

Our Black Ancestry

A 35K+ Facebook group started in 2007 by Sharon Morgan, it includes a compilation of research links that are designed to take you straight to sources that will be useful for you as the Black researcher. **https://ourblackancestry.com**

The Schomburg Center for Research in Black Culture

While not a genealogical site per se, the Schomburg is a world-leading cultural institution devoted to the research, preservation, and exhibition of materials focused on African American, African Diaspora, and African experiences. **www.drupal.nypl.org/locations/schomburg**

The Global Experience of Being Black

Created by Dr. Abdul Alkalimat, a Black scholar and activist—and one of the founders of the Black Studies movement, this webliography addresses the question: What is the African Diaspora? What does it mean to be Black in the world today? Who is Black? What is the relationship between being Black and having a specific nationality, language, or parents? What does "race" (biology) have to do with it? A comprehensive 285-link, 82-plus-country look at the global Black experience includes data, culture, youthful self-expression. One new genre is young Black women profiling countries on their own YouTube channels — insightful and fun. **www.alkalimat.org/global/**

Chapter 23

General Genealogy Sites

Family Search

Over a billion digitized images and millions of indexed names can be accessed for free on the FamilySearch website of the Church of Jesus Christ of Latter-day Saints (LDS or Mormons). In many cases, indexed transcriptions can be searched to locate available records, but don't miss the millions of digitized images available only by browsing. Records are available from various locations and include data like census records from the U.S., Argentina, and Mexico. The site is also accessible in many different languages. **Familysearch.org**

International Genealogical Index

A partial index to vital records from around the world, the IGI database contains birth, marriage, and death records from various locations including: Africa, Asia, Great Britain, the Caribbean Islands, Mexico, Central America, the United States, Canada, and South America. In the IGI, you can find dates and places of births, christenings, and marriages for more than 285 million deceased people. Many of the names were extracted from original records from the early 1500s to the early 1900s. Free database at **Familysearch.org/search/collection/igi**

Relative Finder

Relative Finder: This site uses data from FamilySearch to show how you are related to other people (to include historical figures). This website is most useful if you are a member of the LDS church, but it is free to everyone. **Relativefinder.org**

My Heritage

This site also has a free genealogy software that allows you to build your family tree online. It's called familytree builder. (**Don't confuse it with familytree maker, which is also a good software program, but expensive). A rapid expansion of its database, now topping 12 billion records, powers email alerts when records match your trees. **You can acquire full record access with unlimited trees for an annual fee. DNA test kits are also available for a cost. **myheritage.com**

Heritage Quest Online

The free genealogy records from the HeritageQuest Online are only available through institutions (like libraries) that subscribe to the service. But if you have a local library card, chances are that you can access it from there. The databases focus on the United States and include digital images of the complete federal census, 1790 to 1930 (with head of household indexes for most years), thousands of family and local history books, and Revolutionary War pension files, plus PERSI, an index to articles in thousands of genealogical journals. Check with your local, college, or state library system to see if they offer access. Most even offer free online access from home — saving you the trip to the library. **Heritagequestonline.com**

RootsWeb

This site allows users to upload, modify, link, and display their family trees to share their work with other researchers. WorldConnect allows people to add, modify, or delete their information at any time. This free genealogy database currently contains more than half a billion names in more than 400,000 family trees, and you can search them all online for absolutely no charge! You can also submit your own family tree information for free. **Wc.rootsweb.com**

U.S. Federal Land Records

The Bureau of Land Management (BLM) provides free online database access to Federal land conveyance records for the Public Land States, as well as images of several million Federal land title records issued between 1820 and 1908 for dozens of federal land states (primarily land west and south of the original thirteen colonies). The website contains images of the documents: land patents, survey plats and fieldnotes, land status records, tract books, etc. **Glorecords.blm.gov**

USGenWeb

A mega-database that began as a volunteer project in Kentucky and grew to include every state in the US. The site is full of free searchable records for each state and county including deeds, wills, census records, cemetery transcriptions, tombstone records and obituaries, and pension collections. **Usgenweb.org**

US Social Security Death Index

The SSDI contains more than 64 million records of U.S. citizens who have died since 1962. From the SSDI you can find the following information: the date of birth, date of death, state where the Social Security number was issued, the individual's residence at time of death and the location where the death benefit was mailed (next of kin). **Socialsecuritydeathindex-search.com**

Ancient Faces

Launched in 2000, the purpose of this site is to share photos and memories of ancestors. This family photo-sharing site has expanded to encompass collaborative biographies, which serve as sort of a Wikipedia entry for the not-necessarily-famous. **Ancientfaces.com**

Geni

This site allows you to create, share, and collaborate with other family members on your family tree. Shared trees at this free site include more than 230 million profiles. **Geni.com**

We Relate

The goal of this website is to build a "unified family tree" to connect us all as the human family. This collaborative tree "wiki," sponsored by the Foundation for On-Line Genealogy, has pages for some three million people. **Werelate.org**

Access Genealogy

This website states that it has "the largest collection of free genealogy for your United States research." The site provides a one-stop shop of thousands of free searchable websites and databases. There are tutorials available to learn how to use the site more effectively. **Accessgenealogy.com**

WikiTree

A collaborative effort by contributors to grow an accurate single human family tree using DNA and traditional genealogical resources. **Wikitree.com**

BYU—Idaho Western State Marriage Index

Many Black families made their way out west, so this website is worth a check if yours ventured that far. Find your ancestors' marriage registry in a database with marriage records for 12 Western states. Arizona, Idaho, and Nevada are best represented. **Abish.byui.edu/specialCollections/westernStates/search**

Genealogy Trails

Launched back in 2000 to transcribe Illinois records, this volunteer site now hosts data for every state plus nationwide finds such as Fanning's Illustrated Gazetteer from 1850, Trail of Tears data, military headstones, and even "chuckwagon" recipes that make use of pioneer-era ingredients. Remember—Black people were pioneers too! **Genealogytrails.com**

Library of Congress

At the Library of Congress (LOC) website, you can find books, documents, archived music and folk traditions, historical photos, and Sanborn fire insurance maps. The LOC has many other databases and digital collections useful to the genealogist. **Loc.gov**

National Archives and Records Administration

Millions of federal records and other documents are available for free. Order veterans' service records, check out old maps and photos, research immigrant arrivals, search WWII enlistments and much more. There are NARA facilities in many large cities. Find the branch nearest to you. **Archives.gov**

The New York Public Library Digital Collections

The NYPL has many thousands of items that you can search for free from the library's collections: maps, photographs, manuscripts, videos, and more. **Digitalcollections.nypl.org**

ACPL Genealogy Center

The nation's second-largest genealogy library, the Allen County Public Library in Fort Wayne, Indiana, offers free collections of Native American, African American, and military records; family Bibles; a surname file; and state resources from Indiana and beyond. **Acpl.lib.in.us**

Reclaim the Record

A website created by a nonprofit activist group who identify important genealogical records that ought to be in the public domain, but which are wrongly restricted by government archives, libraries, and agencies. More than 30 million records have been reclaimed so far and are searchable for free on the site. **Reclaimtherecords.org**

Tribal Pages

This site helps you build, maintain, and share your family tree online. Pick your own privacy level here; if you choose, only invited family members can view or update your tree. Create charts, publish, and share family stories, and even send customized newsletters to your kin. Basic trees are free; posting more than 1,000 photos and certain other features require a paid subscription. **Tribalpages.com**

Dead Fred

This genealogy photo archive has helped thousands of people find pictures of their ancestors. It's free to search the archive of nearly 150,000 records representing 22,000 surnames, plus "mystery" pics. Paying members get various customization options and enhanced photo-posting. **Deadfred.com**

Family Tree Searcher

A one-stop shop to search for your ancestors at the major websites that have family trees. You can check up to ten sites, from Ancestry.com to World Connect by entering your ancestor's data just once. A manual search option adds hints and suggestions for all the linked sites. **Familytreesearcher.com**

Guild of One-Name Studies

A website with free online indexes to many types of records—many of which are unique to the guild. You can search hundreds of studies covering thousands of surnames (last names) and find related historical and educational resources. Some projects now include DNA components, while others detail surname geographic distribution and origins. **One-name.org**

The Legal Genealogist

Genealogy from a legal perspective. Find answers to your questions about copyright and old photos, DNA, record access, cemeteries, and more . **Legalgenealogist.com**

RootsTech

Attend more than 1,500 sessions across 20-plus categories from this free virtual genealogy conference sponsored by FamilySearch. The latest additions include presentations from the all-digital March 2022 conference. **Familysearch.org**

Internet Archive

Digital discoveries await here, including old books, family and local histories, and media of all types. Or check the "Wayback Machine," which searches the history of over 673 billion pages on the internet. **Archive.org**

One-Step Webpages

Stephen Morse, a computer programmer turned genealogist, developed a large database to help search major federal records collections. **Stevemorse.org**

Fulton History

At over 49 million newspaper pages, this site is pretty impressive. Most of the papers are based in New York and cover the U.S. and Canada. **www.fultonhistory.com**

Chronicling America

The Library of Congress's database of historic newspapers. **https://chroniclingamerica.loc.gov**

Ellis Island Database

A great database for immigrants who arrived to the United States through Ellis Island, New York. **libertyellisfoundation.org/passenger**

Some Genealogy Research Libraries

Your Local Family History Center

This may be the single best-kept secret on the planet…the Church of Latter-Day Saints (LDS) has really helped to make genealogy accessible to almost everyone. The Genealogical Society of Utah (GSU) was established in 1894, and in 1938, began to microfilm records which contained genealogical data from around the world, and today this microfilm makes up much of the library's collection. Over time the GSU morphed into FamilySearch and is currently working on digitizing many of its microfilm collections to be shared online. Although the main purpose of the library had a lot to do with the

LDS's religious beliefs, you don't have to be a member of the LDS to use its resources to research your family history. The church's Family History Library, located in downtown Salt Lake City, Utah, is a five-story genealogical research facility that is run by FamilySearch and is open to the public. However, there are also branches of the FHL called Family History Centers that are all over the country—even in cities you might not think they'd be! While there are over 4,400 FHCs operating in more than 134 countries there are only about 17 major regional branch library-class facilities. The others are ward, branch, and stake facilities with at least one or more genealogical computers. All of which are free to you! **familysearch.org/centers/locations**

Some other research libraries (not affiliated with the LDS church) are:

<u>Moorland-Spingarn Research Center</u>

Located on the Howard University campus in Washington D.C., you'll find a plethora of primary source material here. **https://dh.howard.edu/msrc**

<u>Clayton Library Center for Genealogical Research</u>

Located in Texas, this library has many databases for the researcher. **https://houstonlibrary.org**

<u>Midwest Genealogy Center</u>

These libraries are located in Missouri and can be accessed at **https:/mymcpl.org/genealogy**

<u>Allen County Public Library</u>

Located in Indiana, this is a powerhouse research facility that can be accessed online. There is also an African American gateway that provides access to records specific to the Black researcher.

www.acpl.lib.in.us/genealogy

Chapter 24

Canada

Canadian Genealogy & Family History

A large collection of Canadian census records from 1640-1926, passenger and border entry lists from 1865-1935, historical military records, and land records that are free to access online. The Library and Archives of Canada (LAC) has several databases for the genealogist researching their family history. **Bac-lac.gc.ca**

Vital Records of British Columbia, Canada

Search for birth, adoption, marriage, divorce, or death registrations in British Columbia, Canada. This free genealogy index covers all births from 1872-1899, marriages from 1872-1924, and deaths from 1872-1979, as well as WWII overseas casualties, colonial marriages (1859-1872) and baptisms (1836-1885). **Ww2.gov.bc.ca**

The Canadian County Atlas Digital Project

The County Atlas Project is a free searchable database of the property owners' names which appear on the township maps in the county atlases. Maps, portraits, and properties have been scanned, with links from the property owners' names in the database. **Digital.library.mcgill.ca**

Library and Archives of Canada

A great resource on the early days of Port Roseway (later renamed Shelburne) and the town founded by free Blacks named Birchtown. **www.bac-lac.gc.ca/eng/discover/mililtary-heritage/loyalists**

Loyalists in the Maritimes

www.bac-lac.gc.ca/eng/discover/mililtary-heritage/loyalists

Book of Negroes

Contained within the British Headquarters papers Microfilm (M369). It provides the names of Black Loyalists and gives physical characteristics like distinguishing marks. It also lists the names of ships that carried them as well as their status (slave or free). **www.bac-lac.gc.ca/eng/discover/mililtary-heritage/loyalists/book-of-negroes**

Chapter 25

Obituaries and Cemeteries

Obituary Daily Times

A daily index of published obituaries from around the world, this free genealogy index grows by approximately 2,500 entries per day, with obituaries dating back to 1995. This is just an index so you would need to go to the source to obtain the actual record. **Obituaries.rootsweb.com**

Interment

This free genealogy database holds more than 25 million records from cemeteries around the world. The website contains actual cemetery transcriptions and burial records as well as links to other cemetery transcriptions available on the internet from cemeteries worldwide and which draws on some unusual sources—fraternal groups, historical societies, and governments—as well as volunteer contributions. **Interment.net**

Billion Graves

Search or browse more than nine million transcribed records (many including photographs) from cemeteries in the United States, Canada, and more than 50 other countries. The volunteer-run site is growing quickly with hundreds of thousands of new cemetery records added each month. It's free to search—or add to—this collection of cemetery data and photos, linked to GPS coordinates. You can also upgrade for an annual fee to search by family plots and nearby graves, plus get priority support. **Billiongraves.com**

Find A Grave

Millions of transcriptions (many with photos) are available for you to search to find the graves of ancestors. Search options include nicknames, and maiden names, and you can create memorials or even place virtual "flowers." **Findagrave.com**

Names In Stone

Search by deceased ancestor or cemetery to get not only tombstone names but also the grave location; you can view the location on an interactive map. Members of the paid plan will get enhanced features, but basic searching is free. **Namesinstone.com**

Nationwide Gravesite Locator

If your military ancestors were buried in VA (Department of Veterans Affairs) National Cemeteries, state veterans' cemeteries, or other US locations (such as those with government grave markers), you can search for them here on this site run by the National Cemetery Administration. **Gravelocator.cem.va.gov/ngl/index.jsp**

Chapter 26
The Caribbean

While there are few websites devoted specifically to vital records from the Caribbean, you can type into any browser a search phrase like, "Barbados baptism records" and a list of sites where those records are located will appear. Most will be on **family search.org** or **ancestry.com**. Additionally, WorldGenWeb has country landing pages where there are links to each country in the world—and various resources inside each link. **www.worldgenweb.org**. Below is a sample of some of the records repositories of the Caribbean.

Anguilla

Births, Deaths and Marriages **www.gov.ai/vitalrecords.htm**

Antigua and Barbuda

National Archives of Antigua **antiguanationalarchives.org**

Bahamas

National Archives of the Bahamas **bahamasnationalarchives.bs/family-history.htm**

Bahamas DNA Project **genealogy.hopetownmuseum.com/bahamasdnaproject/**

Bahamas Historical Society **www.facebook.com/242historical society/**

Resources for Bahamas Genealogy **bahamianbib.blogspot.com/2006/03/bibliography-of-bahami an-genealogy.html**

Barbados

Trace your ancestors **www.barbadosancestors.com**

Barbados National Archives **www.visitbarbados.org/archives-department**

Barbados Museum and Historical Society **www.visitbarbados.org/barbados-museum-historical-s ociety**

Bermuda

Bermuda National Library **www.bml.bm**

Cayman Islands

Cayman Islands National Archive **www.cina.gov.ky/**

Cuba

Cuban National Archives **www.ecured.cu/Archivo_Nacional_de_Cuba**

Dominica

National Documentation Centre and National Archives www.dlis.gov.dm/National-documentaiton-centre

Registry Division (goes back to 1861) www.nationalsecurity.gov.dm/divisions/registry-division

Dominican Republic

National Genealogical Institute www.idg.org.do/enlaces-idg.htm

National Archive www.agn.dob.do

Grenada

National Archives www.grenadanationalarchives.wordpress.com

Guadeloupe

National Archives www.archivesguadeloupe.fr

Haiti

Genealogy Association of Haiti www.agh.qc.ca/indexen.html

Jamaica

Afro-Caribbean Institute of Jamaica   https://acij.ioj.org.jm

The Jamaican Historical Society https:/jamaicanhistorical.tripod.com

Netherlands Antilles, St. Eustatius, St. Maarten and Bonaire, Aruba and Saba

Records for these locations can be found at the free Dutch genealogy site Genlias www.genlias.nl

Aruban National Archives
https://www.government.aw/governance-administration/aruban-national-archives-ana_45660/#:~:text=The%20Aruban%20National%20Archives%20(ANA,cultural%20heritage%20'%20of%20our%20island

U.S. Virgin Islands

These islands, which encompass St. Thomas, St. Croix and St. John, were known as the Danish West Indies prior to 1917. Therefore, most pre-1917 records are in the Danish national archives (and on FHL microfilm). After 1917, the islands belonged to the United States and so are in U.S. records repositories. The Danish Demographic Database has transcribed St. Croix census records. https://ddd.dda.dk/soeg_stcroix.html

Danish State Archive https://www.sa.dk/da/

Chapter 27
England & Wales

Free Census for the United Kingdom

Search for free in this comprehensive name index to more than 32 million individuals who lived in Scotland, England, Ireland, and Wales in the 19th century. This genealogy index includes the individual's name, age, place of birth, and occupation. **Freecen.org.uk**

Free BMD

An ongoing project aiming to transcribe the Civil Registration index of births, marriages, and deaths for England and Wales. **Freebmd.org.uk**

Free Reg

A site dedicated to providing free internet searches of baptism, marriage, and burial records from UK parishes, nonconformists records and other relevant sources. **Freereg.org.uk**

Debt of Honour Register

Provided by the Commonwealth War Graves Commission, this website allows you to search for personal and service details and places of commemoration for the 1.7 million members of the Commonwealth forces (including the United Kingdom and former colonies) who died in the First or Second World Wars, as well as a record of some 60,000 civilian casualties of the Second World War provided without details of burial location. The cemeteries and memorials where these names are commemorated are located in over 150 countries. **Cwgc.org**

Museums In Liverpool

From the 1700s, Liverpool was a port city with a diverse population from around the world. It is home to the oldest Black community in the United Kingdom dating to 1730. Some can trace their lineage back ten generations—they are the descendants of seamen, traders and freed slaves. Any person who entered England after 1722 was considered free. Liverpool has several museums that explore aspects of the Black experience. There is the National Museum and the International Slavery Museum. **www.liverpoolmuseums.org.uk**

Chapter 28
Global Sites

WorldGenWeb

The WorldGenWeb project began with the stated goal of having "every country in the world represented by an online website" and also hosted by local researchers. The site provides links to free genealogy information and free transcribed genealogy records. **worldgenweb.org**

World Cat

Any book written that is still available and in print can be found via this website. More than two billion items cataloged here—with details on the nearest library (to you) that has it. Once you find it, submit an interlibrary loan request at your local library and it can be sent there for you to pick up. **Worldcat.org**

Chapter 29
Software Programs

Ancestral Quest Basics

This free program connects to two genealogy sites—Rootsweb and Ancestry. While you can upload photos, the free version doesn't allow you to create ancestor charts. **Ancquest.com**

Family Tree Builder

This program is owned by MyHeritage DNA. You aren't limited to only adding information about ancestors; you can upload facts, notes, sources, and multimedia such as photos, sound, and video clips. You can also import your family tree from other sites. **Myheritage.com/family-tree-builder**

Genealogical Research and Analysis Management Program Systems

Gramps, as this program is affectionately known, is one of the best free programs with many reports, charts, and features—like the ability to handle international letters and characters. The downside is that the program may not be easy to install. **Gramps-project.org**

Legacy Family Tree

This is a favorite among genealogists because of its simple design, robust program, and plentiful features. **Legacyfamilytree.com**

RootsMagic Essentials

This is a great software program for the beginner. The interface is easy to understand and navigate. **Rootsmagic.com/try/rootsmagic**

Trello

This is not a genealogy program, but a free online collaboration tool organizes projects and ideas into easy-to-navigate boards, lists and cards. There are articles online to help you set up Trello to use for your research. **www.trello.com**

Finally, Microsoft Office has family tree templates that can be downloaded.

templates.office.com/en-us/photo-family-tree-tm88904269

FAMILY TREE

Ancestral family tree up to three generations

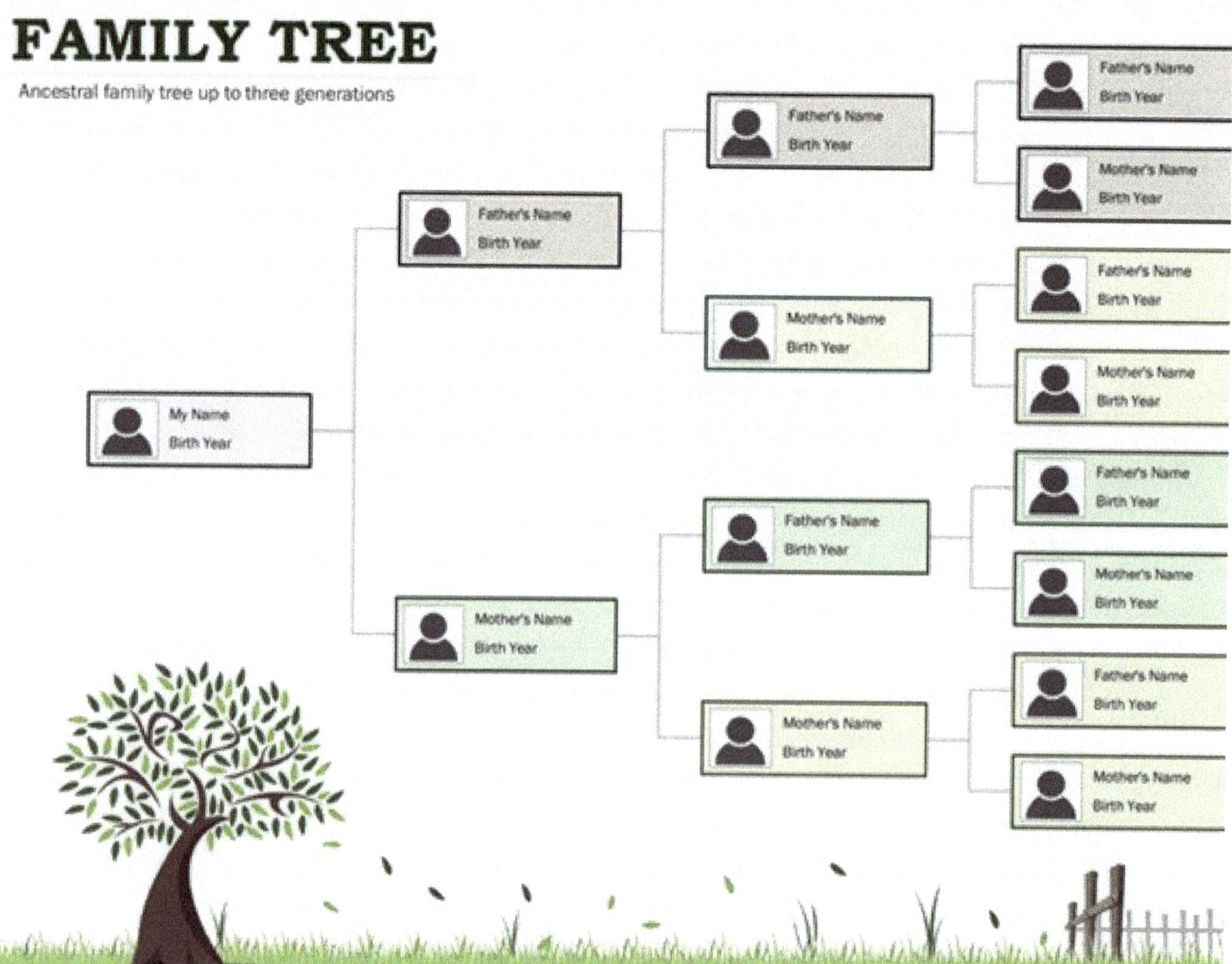

Chapter 30
Subscriber Sites

Fold3.com Black History Collection

View more than a million rare photos and documents. **www.Gofold3.com/blackhistory?iid=1343**

Find My Past

Recent interface improvements, including image thumbnails and viewing controls, make it even easier to access this subscription site. Coverage is strongest for the British Isles—boosted by the addition of ten million Scottish parish vital records—though US and Australian records have recently been augmented. The site also provides testing via its LivingDNA test kit. For extra pay-per-view fees, the 1921 census of England and Wales is available here. **Findmypast.com**

American Ancestors

A database sponsored by the New England Historic Genealogical Society, this subscription site is an online repository for over one billion searchable records. **Americanancestors.org**

Genealogical

A website run by the Genealogical Publishing Company, which has published more than 2,000 books ranging from transcriptions of old records not available elsewhere to tomes that are standards in the field of genealogy. An annual ePub subscription offers digital access to hundreds of titles. **Genealogical.com**

Roots Point

For us, probably the most useful collection on this site is the state histories database, although the site does contain other records collections like immigration records. You can join with an annual fee or try the site for a small charge. **Rootspoint.com**

Newspapers

You can often get access to this vast repository through an ancestry.com account. It has over 280M digitized newspapers, so it's worth paying a subscription when you want to comb through old newspapers. **newspapers.com**

Chapter 31

DNA Test Sites

This is not a comprehensive list of all the DNA test kits that are on the market. These are just the most popular for genealogical use. Check the fine print. If you are under 18, most companies require that you have the explicit consent of your parent or legal guardian to submit a DNA sample.

African Ancestry

This DNA testing company was co-founded by African American Dr. Gina Paige. Probably the most expensive test but also the most detailed as it is supposed to be able to pinpoint not only the region, but also the tribe of your African ancestors. **Africanancestry.com**

MyHeritageDNA

Founded by Israeli entrepreneur Gilad Japhet, these tests run $89 each, but can often be found on sale. They also happen to be one of the more comprehensive tests available—as they test many more markers (more on that in Chapter 33). **www.myheritage.com**

23 and Me

Founded by Anne Wojcicki, 23andMe provides both health reports and ancestry-only kits. It also has more than ten million DNA testers, making it worth a look for matching relatives. Its family tree feature automatically generates a visualization of genetic matches who have opted in. You have a choice of doing the full health testing, or the ancestry-only test kit. **23andme.com**

Ancestry

The AncestryDNA test has refined its ethnicity estimates, with more than 1,500 genetic communities represented. **Ancestry.com**

Family Tree DNA

This popular testing company claims, "the world's most comprehensive DNA matching database for autosomal DNA, Y-DNA and mtDNA." Family Tree DNA tests for all three and kits range in price. **Familytreedna.com**

Chapter 32

DNA Information Sites

GEDMatch

This site allows you to share and compare your DNA results with others. You can upload your data from any test kit you've taken and use any of the site's many DNA tools to work. **Gedmatch.com**

Through the Trees

Run by genealogy expert Shannon Christmas, this blog explores new tools and technologies in genetic genealogy. **https://throughthetreesblog.tumblr.com**

DNAeXplained

This blog explains the finer points of DNA techniques and methods to help you understand exactly what it's all about. **Dna-explained.com**

International Society of Genetic Genealogy Wiki

A great site that provides answers to your DNA questions for free. Search the 700-plus expert articles at this group's site. **Isogg.org/wiki**

Your DNA Guide

This site can help you understand exactly what kinds of questions a DNA test kit can answer. **Yourdnaguide.com**

*Again, this is not a comprehensive list of sites—just some that I have found to be helpful.

Chapter 33

A Note About DNA Tests

But first, the Micro Genetics Lesson

In case I haven't said this already, genetics can be used to help you research your family history. Genetics is the scientific study of genes and heredity. DNA embodies generations of all of our ancestors-whether they are from 30 years ago, 500, or 4000.

There are three types of DNA—autosomal, mitochondrial, and Y-DNA. Every human being receives a set of 22 chromosomes: half from the mother, and half from the father. These are called autosomes, because they are always the same 22 chromosomes (even though there are variations inside them). Autosomal DNA recombines (or gets newly mixed up) every generation. This is why it's possible for you and your brother to each take a DNA test and get slightly different calculations of ethnicity—even though you both come from the same set of parents. For example, my ethnic makeup includes about 30% Nigerian DNA and 5% Irish DNA (among a lot of other stuff), and my brother's ethnic makeup is assessed at 38% Nigerian DNA and no Irish DNA. It's just the luck of the draw as to what your ethnic makeup will be—even between full-blood siblings.

Mitochondrial DNA, or mt-DNA, is DNA that is inherited from your mother as it is passed down **only** through the female line. It is essentially a direct maternal history that goes back thousands of years. There are about 16,569 base pairs of mitochondrial DNA. There are some mutations—but overall, it remains the same. Mitochondria supply a cell's energy, so organs affected by abnormal mitochondria are those that require a lot of energy—like the brain, heart, and liver. Mt-DNA is passed from a mother to al her children, so both males and females can take Mt-DNA tests. However, males cannot pass on mt-DNA to their children.

The 23rd chromosome is the biological sex expression chromosome. If you are (or were) born with a female genetic sex expression, or in other words, a biological female, that means you received an "X" chromosome from both your mother and your father. If you were born with a male genetic sex expression (or biologically male), that means you received an "X" chromosome from your mother and a "Y" chromosome from your father. Only men have the "Y" chromosome and male DNA tends to pass relatively unchanged through the male line. DNA tests on the market today will provide results for either autosomal DNA, mitochondrial DNA, or Y-DNA samples. But not all three at the same time. Mt-DNA and Y-DNA are also called unparental histories because they do not recombine or remix ever.

Your (or any living thing's) complete set of DNA is called the genome. You may have heard of the Human Genome Project? It was an international project that started in the 1990s and was completed in 2003. Scientists basically used the DNA of a sample population and created a generic DNA sequence map (generic in the sense that it isn't based on just one person's DNA). The study of the human genome is called genomics. Just about every cell in your body contains a complete copy of the over three billion (yes three billion) DNA base pairs that make up the human genome. These base pairs are also identified as letters— "A" for adenine, ""C" for cytosine, "G" for guanine, and "T" for thymine. So yes, the genetic code in each person is a combination of those four letters—A, C, G, and T.[1]

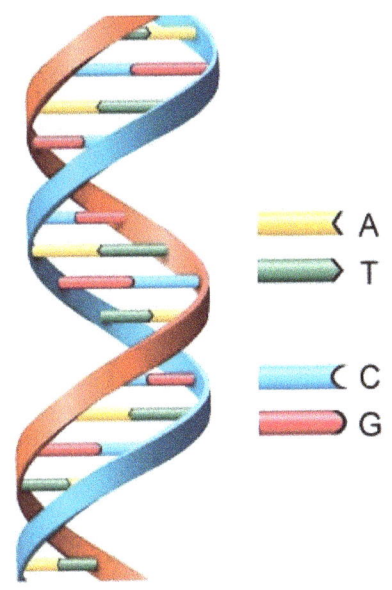

A

T

C

G

However, DNA degrades and mutates over time. We know all ready that all people come from Africa. Over time, as people migrated to other parts of the world, some of the genes they carried with them changed over time. Genes do become more diverse over time, which is a concept known as genetic drift. Genetic drift happens in every population—some genes may not survive a generation while other genes become dominant depending on any number of factors. It's all totally random. This is why all populations from Sweden to China carry varying amounts of African DNA, because we all come from the same place. Fascinating, isn't it?

The Human Genome Project revealed that there are about 20,5000 human genes.

Autosomal DNA informs relatedness—which is another way of saying that autosomal DNA tells you how you are related (or not related) to someone else. The more pieces of matching genetic code you share with someone, the higher the likelihood that you are related to them.

DNA Testing Basics

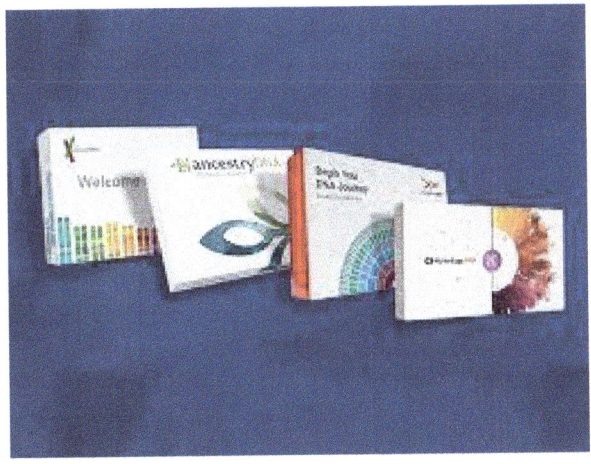

DNA kits[2] test your DNA to determine your ethnic makeup. The science (genetics) is getting better all the time and can often narrow down a region inside of a country. Unfortunately, most of the commercial kits off the shelf cannot tell you which tribe in Africa you descend from. However, as more people of African descent are tested, the larger the databases are from which scientists can draw inferences. It is important to note that each testing company handles privacy differently. None of them are supposed to reveal your information to law enforcement without your consent. Some companies do an "opt-in" while some have "opt-out". So just make sure you've read and understand exactly what you've agreed to. Even with the possibility of law enforcement getting their hands on our information, I still think the benefits of DNA tests outweigh the drawbacks. Diseases that are endemic in our culture—sickle cell anemia, diabetes, etc., need to be thoroughly researched using our DNA. A recent study showed that cases of type 2 diabetes have risen dramatically over the last ten years and the victims are often Black kids. Type 2 is more aggressive and the results show up a lot more quickly—blindness, amputation, etc. We've got to have more of our people involved in clinical studies, but we also have to have more of our DNA available to research.

Additionally, you must manually opt in to allowing your DNA to be researched for medical purposes. Geneticists and doctors study DNA to look for causes and cures of various diseases. So allowing your DNA to be studied is a tremendous help. Think about it: if all the test samples are from people of European descent, how can we know how different treatments and medicines will affect people of color?

It is very true that in the past, Black and brown people often had very good reasons for not trusting medicine and science[3], but at least in that area, times have changed. Science seems committed to being more inclusive in order to better treat people of all ethnicities. There are some studies that suggest that the human genome has changed more in the past 5000 years than previously thought. Using deep sequencing, scientists were able to determine where one letter (remember the four we mentioned earlier?) in the DNA sequence was different--suggesting a variant. It also turns out that most of the variants—including those that are harmful—were developed in the past 5000-10000 years.[4]

DNA kits connect you to other relatives in your family who have taken the tests. But there are a few things to be aware of when you take a DNA test. For one thing, it can only reliably go back between eight and twelve generations. Remember when we said that DNA degrades over time? That means that when you try to search for relatives beyond that, the DNA can be tricky…or nonexistent. Just understand that a DNA test is not the end all of your family history research. In fact, you have many more genealogical ancestors than genetic ancestors. Using my earlier example about me and my brother, what if my brother assumed he had no Irish relatives simply because he had no Irish DNA? This is why you have to do the genealogical research. It is much more conclusive.

When you take a test and upload your results to sites like MyHeritage or 23&Me, the platform will provide you with names of people who have also taken that test who are a genetic match with you. Just know that whatever test you take, when you upload your results, they are only going to match up with other people who have uploaded their data to that site as well. So to cast the widest net and get the most potential DNA matches, it's a good idea to upload your data to aggregate collectors (also known as universal translators) like GEDMATCH—where data from most testing sites can be uploaded. Also, remember that out of your 3.2 billion base pairs (your genome), these sites are only testing about 7000 "markers" called SNPs—single nucleotide polymorphisms (pronounced snips—an oddly accurate acronym). I'm not great at math, but even I can see that that is a tiny amount of DNA that is being studied. So those percentages of ethnicity I mentioned earlier are based on the number of markers tested, not your entire genome. And they are assessing *similarity*—not necessarily *ancestry*. In other words, they take your DNA and match it up with the DNA of other representative populations of people who have taken DNA tests, and compare to see where and how you match up. This is why we say that it is not a definitive reflection of ancestry. This is another reason why it is so very important that more Afro-descendant and African people take DNA tests. We need more and better representative populations to match to our DNA.

I know this is a lot to digest. But really, it's only the tip of the iceberg. My hope is that you might find all of this so interesting that you decide to become a clinical molecular geneticist, or a research computational biologist, or an anthropological geneticist, or a clinical pharmacologist. We desperately need more scientists of color. And don't let anyone tell you that you aren't smart enough to do it!

---

1. The "rungs" of the "ladder" are the DNA pairs. C always matches with G, and A always matches with T. The sides of the ladder are made of sugar and phosphate. They are held together by hydrogen bonds.
Note: Scientists use the term "double helix" to describe the spiral physical structure of DNA.
2. If you are under 18, you must have your parent or guardian's permission to take a DNA test.
3. The Tuskegee Experiment and Henrietta Lacks' story come to mind.
4. Scientists have also been able to determine when European and African populations diverged--which basically means when Africans migrated from Africa to Europe.

Chapter 34
Final Words of Wisdom

Whoa...this is a lot of information! We know. Take your time with this handbook. Start slow. This isn't a sprint but a marathon that will take you around the world. And we are in it for the long haul. Never ever ever be afraid to ask questions. And if the people who are supposed to help you find answers can't help you (or won't), tackle it again another day and another way. Don't ever let anyone intimidate you into giving up. This is true for genealogy and anything else.

And please do not assume that anyone else's family tree will be thoroughly researched. Many people add names to their trees that may or may not be actual relatives. So no shortcuts—do the work to establish the relationship. Don't just cut and paste from the family trees of other people. Also, remember that not every source will yield information that is useful to you—and know that you might spend time and money to find an answer that just doesn't materialize. This is true for every genealogist.

For the Black genealogist, remember that the best sources for you will be:

· Family members first

· Local church histories, conference programs, etc.

· Historic Black Colleges & Universities (HBCUs)

· Deeds, claims, bills of sale, etc., at the local county or city courthouse

· Vital Records: Every city and/or county has a place where vital records (marriage, birth, death) are kept. Many of them are now   online

· Federal census records

· Freedmen's Bureau records (to include Freedmen's Savings & Trust Co.)

· African American newspapers of the 1800s and 1900s

The rest of the pages in this book are for you to record some recipes, family stories, bits of information, etc.

One last note before you go forth and research. No matter what, make sure you always do four things:

1. Honor your ancestors. They are the reason you are here. And if no one else ever tells you this, I, for one, am very happy that you are here. Because you are unique, and you were put on this Earth to do something great. Let your genealogical research help you find both your heritage and your destiny, which is the divine work that you were born to do.

2. Always be thinking about what you want your descendants to know or remember about you.

3. Spell genealogy correctly...just sayin'…

4. HAVE FUN!

MAKE ART.
MAKE FOOD.
MAKE MOVIES.
MAKE MEMORIES.
MAKE CONNECTIONS.
MAKE FAMILY HISTORY.

LIVE IN JOY

Chapter 35

Glossary

Adinkra: a writing system incorporating symbols representing various concepts that is used by the Akan peoples of Ghana to mark fabrics, walls, pottery, and other surfaces.

Ancestor: A person, typically more remote than a grandparent, whom is a direct blood relative.

Ancestry: Family lineage – one's family or ethnic descent.

Archive: A place where public records or historical documents are kept.

Border entry: The location on land where new immigrants first enter a country. Cemetery Records: Records related to a deceased person's burial (both office records and tombstone inscriptions)

Census: An official recording of information about individuals living within a household. These were compiled everyten years startingin 1790, and provide specific information about everyone within a house or dwelling.

Christening: In most churches this refers to the baptism of babies. Churches usually keep a record of each christening, and family members and godparents who attended.

Church/Temple/Synagogue Records: Records kept by religious institutions of parishioners (church members), including marriage certificates, baptisms, confirmations, burials, birth records, school attendance, and other materials.

Citation: A reference that links the information cited to a source (the originator of the information) to ensure traceability.

Candomblé: An African-based religion of South America that involves the veneration of spirits known as orixás. Deriving their names and attributes from traditional West African gods, they are equated with Roman Catholic saints. Various myths are told about these orixás, which are regarded as subservient to a transcendent creator deity, Oludumaré. Each individual is believed to have a guardian orixá who has been connected to them since before birth and who informs their personality.

Country of origin: The country in which a person is born.

Culture: The arts, beliefs, habits, institutions, and other human endeavors considered together as being characteristic of a particular community, people, or nation.

Debarkation: Departure from a vessel or aircraft.

Descendant: A person that is descended from a particular ancestor; to be a direct blood relative of a specific ancestors.

DNA: The carrier of genetic information that is hereditary and shared across generations of family members.

Embarkation: Boarding a vessel or aircraft or setting out on a journey.

Emigrant: A person who voluntarily leaves a country to live in another.

Enumeration: The process of counting people as for a census.

Family group sheet: A form designed for the recording of basic birth, marriage, and death information about members of a single family.

Family history: The reconstruction (oral or written) of the daily lives of a person's ancestors based on information gathered.

Family tree: A chart that shows how people in a family are related to each other.

Fon: A member of a tribe of people inhabiting the southern part of Benin.

Genealogy: The study of family ancestries and histories, and the collection of information (names, dates) about that family.

Generation: People born about the same time and related to a person at the same level (parents, grandparents, great-grandparents). A period of approximately 30 years separates each generation.

Given name: The (first) name parents give their child at birth.

Griot: An African keeper of the family history. The tradition originated in the 13th century in the Mende empire of Mali. (Mande was the language spoken in the region)

Geechee: An English creole spoken by some black people in parts of North and South Carolina, Georgia, and Florida.

Gullah: A descendant of enslaved Africans living on the coast of North and South Carolina, Georgia, and Florida.

Igbo: A member of a tribe of people of southeastern Nigeria.

Ju-Ju: Juju or ju-ju is a spiritual belief system in the Bahamas that incorporates objects, such as amulets, and spells used in religious practicethat originated in West Africa by the people of Ghana, Nigeria, and Cameroon.

Land Records: Deeds, mortgages, and other records dealing with the buying and selling of property; they often show ownership, location, and description.

Immigrant: A person who enters into anew country to settle there.

Ìṣẹ̀ṣe: The Yoruba indigenous religion that holds that all human beings possess what is known as "Àyànmọ́", which is regarded as destiny or fate. Every person is expected to eventually become one in spirit with Olodumaré (also known as Olorun, the divine creator and source of all energy). Furthermore, the thoughts and actions of each person in Ayé (the physical realm) interact with all other living things, including the Earth. Yoruba religious beliefs are part of Itàn (history), the total complex of songs, histories, stories, and other cultural concepts which make up the Yoruba society.

Maiden name: A woman's family name (surname) before marriage. Some women keep their maiden names after marriage, while others take their husband's surname.

Maternal: A relative that is related on the mother's side of the family.

Migration: Movement from one place to another.

Matrilineal: Of or based on kinship with the mother or the female line.

Military Records: Records generated as a result of an individual's involvement in the armed forces, including draft registration cards, service records, pension records, and bounty land records.

Naturalization Records: Records generated through the process of an individual applying for and becoming a citizen of a country.

Obeah: The practice of Obeah in Jamaica originated from the Ashanti and Koromantin tribes of Africa on the Gold Coast, and is the belief that one can use certain spirits or supernatural agents to work good or evil to the living. The British used the term Obeah to describe all slave acts and practices that were considered supernatural or evil in nature, such as rituals and fetishes.

Obituary: A notice of a death, especially found in newspapers, which includes a biography of the person.

Orisha: (Yoruba "Òrìṣà", Brazilian "Orixá") A deity, or deified ancestor, in Yoruba religion. They are intermediaries between humankind and the supernatural.

Passenger List: Records generated in the tracking of individuals arriving or departing a country. Passenger records have changed over time with different questions being asked through varying periods of immigration.

Patent: An official document showing the transfer of public land to an individual (also known as a grant).

Paternal: A relative that is related on the father's side of the family.

Point of entry: The first place (border entry or port) immigrants arrive when entering a country.

Port: A city or town having a harbor where ships or boats take on or unload cargo or passengers.

Patrilineal: Relating to or based on relationship to the father or descent through the male line.

Pedigree Chart: The display used to show a person's ancestors by listing their parents, their parents' parents, and so on.

Probate Records: Records and documents created during the settling of a person's estate, regardless of whether a person left a will.

Rastafari: A religious and socio-political movement originating in Jamaica that teaches the eventual redemption of Black people and their return to Africa.

Relative: A person connected to a family by birth or marriage.

Santeria: A pantheistic Afro-Cuban folk religion developed from the beliefs and customs of the Yoruba peopleand incorporating some elements of the Catholic religion.

Shango: Shango (Yoruba language: Sàngó, also known as Changó or Xangô in Latin America; and as Jakuta (Cuba) or Badé is an Orisha who is represented by thunder and lightning. Like all of the Yoruba gods (orishas), Shango is both a deified ancestor and a natural force, both aspects being associated with a cult and a priesthood. The religion is practiced in Trinidad, Grenada, and Recife (Brazil).

Sibling: A person's brother or sister.

Spouse: A person legally married to another person.

Surname: A person's family name (last name).

Vital Records (civil registrations): These records refer to civil / governmental (rather than religious) registrations of births, marriages, and deaths.

Yoruba: A member of an African tribe of people located in southwestern Nigeria and Benin.

Chapter 36

Family Heritage Sheets - Parent 1

_____Family Heritage

(Your parent's surname here)

Parent's Full Name

Born in (City, State, or Country)

Moved to _____ (in U.S.) on _____(Date) at age_____

S/He attended school at:

(Elementary)

(Secondary)

(College/Trade School)

S/He played these sports/instruments:

S/He was a member of these clubs:

S/He had these hobbies:

Her/His family attended this church:

Her/His favorite foods are:

Her/His least favorite foods are:

Other notes: (i.e., health issues, languages spoken at home, interests, jobs held, career goals, etc.)

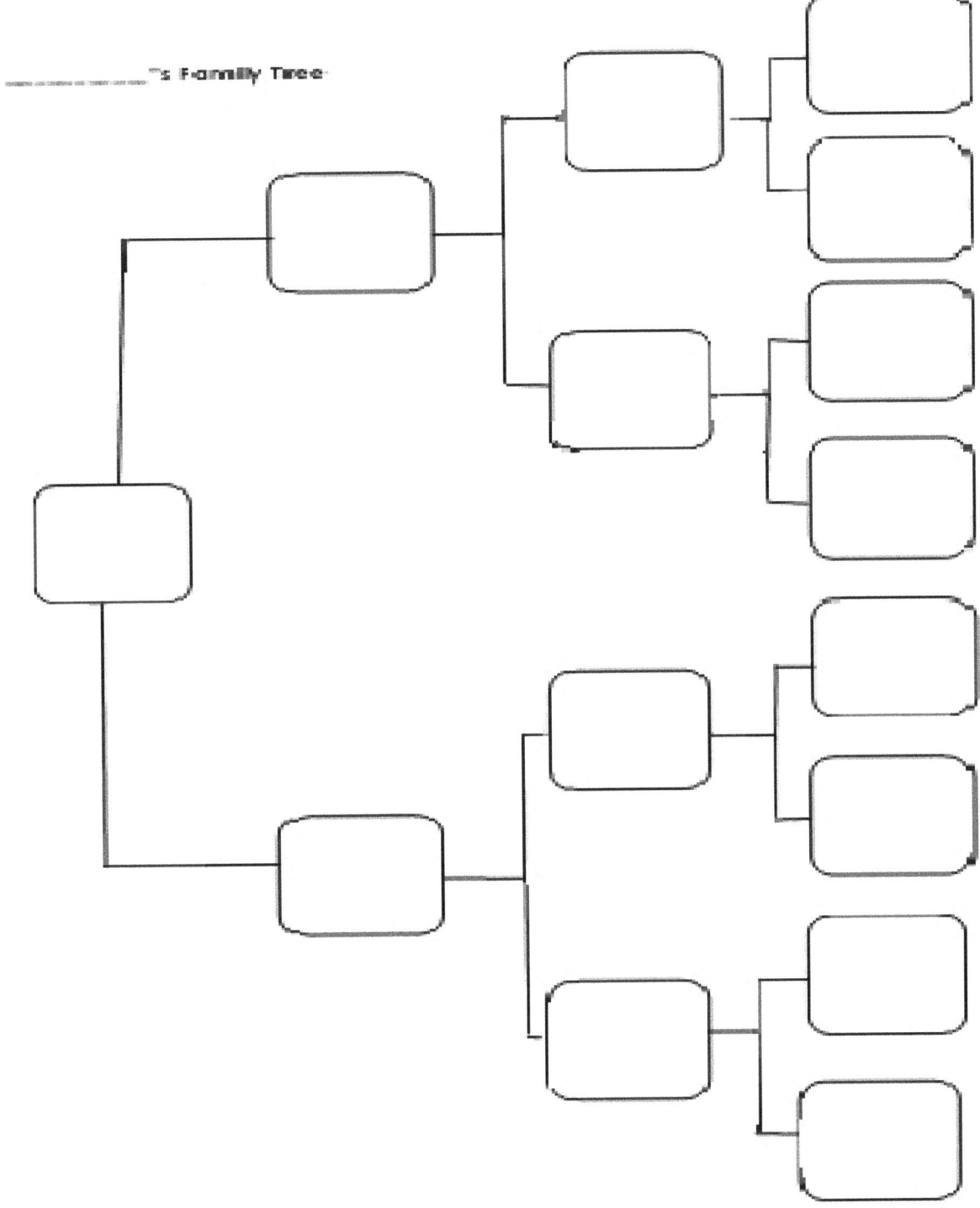

's Family Tree

Cemeteries Where _____'s Family Are Buried
(Your parent's name here)

1.

Name of relative:

Name of site:

Full Address:

Website:

Telephone:

Email address:

2.

Name of site:

Name of relative:

Full Address:

Website:

Telephone:

Email address:

3.

Name of site:

Name of relative:

Full Address:

Website:

Telephone:

Email address:

_____'s Brothers & Sisters

(Your parent's name here)

1.

Name:

Birthdate: Location:

Marriage: Location:

Spouse: Place of birth:

Child:

Child:

Child:

Deceased:

2.

Name:

Birthdate: Location:

Marriage: Location:

Spouse: Place of birth:

Child:

Child:

Child:

Deceased:

3.

Name:

Birthdate: Location:

Marriage: Location:

Spouse: Place of birth:

Child:

Child:

Child:

Deceased:

_____'s Mother's (Your Grandparent's) Family
Heritage

Full Name (Grandparent)

Born in (City, State, or Country)

Moved to _____ (in U.S.) on _____(Date) at
age_____

She attended school at:
(Elementary)
(Secondary)
(College/Trade School)
She played these sports/instruments:

She was a member of these clubs:

She had these hobbies:

Her family attended this church:

Her favorite foods are:

Her least favorite foods are:

Other notes: (i.e., health issues, languages spoken at home, interests, jobs held, career goals, etc.)

_____'s Father's (Your
Grandparent's) Family Heritage

(Your parent's name here)

Full Name (Grandparent)

Born in (City, State, or Country)

He attended school at:

(Elementary)

(Secondary)

(College/Trade School)

He played these sports/instruments:

He was a member of these clubs:

He had these hobbies:

His family attended this church:

His favorite foods are:

His least favorite foods are:

Other notes: (i.e., health issues, languages spoken at home, interests, jobs held, career goals, etc.)

The Griot Corner – _____'s Family Stories, Traditions, and Culture

The Calabash – Recipes from _____'s Family: Ingredients & Instructions

Chapter 37

Family Heritage Sheets- Parent 2

_____ Family Heritage

(Your parent's name here)

Full Name

Born in (City, State, or Country)

Moved to _____ (in U.S.) on _____(Date) at
age_____

S/He attended school at:

(Elementary)

(Secondary)

(College/Trade School)

S/He played these sports/instruments:

S/He was a member of these clubs:

S/He had these hobbies:

Her/His family attended this church:

Her/His favorite foods are:

Her/His least favorite foods are:

Other notes: (i.e., health issues, languages spoken at home, interests, jobs held, career goals, etc.)

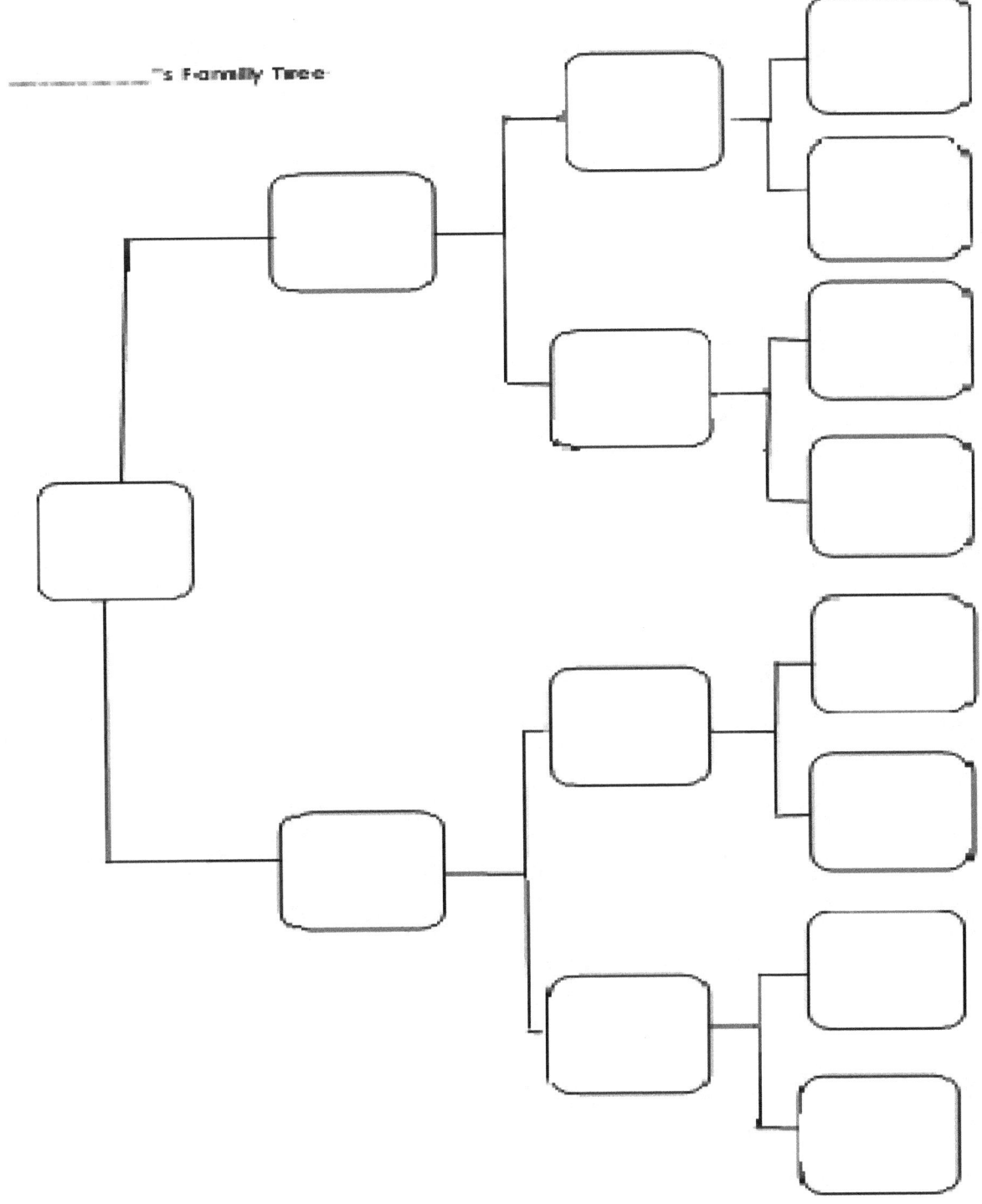

_____'s Family Tree

Cemeteries Where _____'s Family Are Buried
(Your parent's name here)

1.

Name of relative:

Name of site:

Full Address:

Website:

Telephone:

Email address:

2.

Name of site:

Name of relative:

Full Address:

Website:

Telephone:

Email address:

3.

Name of site:

Name of relative:

Full Address:

Website:

Telephone:

Email address:

_____'s Mother's (Your Grandparent's) Family Heritage

(Your parent's name here)

Full Name (Grandparent)

Born in (City, State, or Country)

Moved to _____ (in U.S.) on _____(Date) at age_____

She attended school at:

(Elementary)

(Secondary)

(College/Trade School)

She played these sports/instruments:

She was a member of these clubs:

She had these hobbies:

Her family attended this church:

Her favorite foods are:

Her least favorite foods are:

Other notes: (i.e., health issues, languages spoken at home, interests, jobs held, career goals, etc.)

_____'s Father's (Your Grandparent's) Family Heritage

(Your parent's name here)

Full Name (Grandparent)

Born in (City, State, or Country)

He attended school at:

(Elementary)

(Secondary)

(College/Trade School)

He played these sports/instruments:

He was a member of these clubs:

—

He had these hobbies:

His family attended this church:

His favorite foods are:

His least favorite foods are:

Other notes: (i.e., health issues, languages spoken at home, interests, jobs held, career goals, etc.)

The Griot Corner – _____'s Family Stories, Traditions, and Culture

The Calabash – Recipes from _____'s Family: Ingredients & Instructions

Epilogue

I hope you enjoyed this book and that it motivates you to begin learning your own family history! If you need more pedigree charts or group sheets, check out my website at www.panafrigen.com. I've uploaded a few there—courtesy of the National Genealogical Society. You can print them out and stick them in this book or fill them in online.

Drop me a line and let me know how your journey progresses at panafrigen@gmail.com.

You can also join the Majani Project at www.majani.org where we will soon be holding monthly meetings to discuss all things genealogy—from the very basic to the more advanced. We'll also be learning how to make animated film shorts and graphic novels of our family history. You don't want to miss that! It's all free and anyone can join.